IN TUNE WITH YOUR DOG

An owner's guide to training and
improving behaviour

To John Holmes whose book, The family dog, it's choice and training, started my quest for more knowledge of the canine mind and to Roy Hunter for daring to be different in his compassionate approach to training.

IN TUNE WITH YOUR DOG

An Owner's Guide to Training and
Improving Behaviour

JOHN ROGERSON

The Northern Centre for Animal Behaviour

Published by
The Northern Centre for Animal Behaviour
East Howle, Ferryhill,
Durham DL17 8SA

Originally published as *Your dog, it's development, behaviour and training*
by
Popular Dogs Publishing Co. Ltd

An imprint of the Random Century Group
20 Vauxhall Bridge Road, London SW1V 2SA

First Published 1988
Reprinted 1989, 1990
revised, updated and reprinted 1997
Copyright © John Rogerson 1988 and 1997

Printed and bound in Great Britain by
St Edmundsbury Press Ltd,
Bury St Edmunds, Suffolk

British Library Cataloguing in Publication Data

Rogerson, John
    Your dog: its development, behaviour
    and training.

    1. Dogs – Training
    I.Title
    636.7'083   SF431

ISBN 0 09 173473 8

CONTENTS

Introduction

Since writing this book a little over ten years ago there have been many changes that have taken place in dog training and behaviour therapy. Even though much has changed, the basic principles involved in selecting, raising and training a dog remain the same. Our ability to understand and communicate with man's best friend now becomes even more important as recent legislation requires owners to be held more responsible for the behaviour of their family pets.

My life has changed a great deal since this book was first published in 1988 and I have now become much more involved in teaching the next generation of trainers and behaviourists the art of communication and greater understanding of dogs in our family homes. As my own understanding has improved I have been able to train dogs quicker and more effectively than ever before and so I found it necessary to revise and update my original work to include the very latest information. After all these years I am still actively involved in dog training and compete regularly with my dogs who are my greatest teachers.

I am often asked questions about training or behaviour problems and always try to see things from the dogs point of view. Even though I can usually give a complete answer to a question it is a sobering thought that even the best answers that I can give are merely guesses. You are therefore invited to read this book and re-examine any questions you may have about your dog. If you then address all of your questions to your dog then I can guarantee that you will always get a true and honest answer.

1

Upbringing

Puppy Selection

It is a sad fact that many people spend far less time and effort in selecting a puppy, that they will own for an average of twelve years, than they would spend on selecting a car, that they will own for less than three years. Many young dogs end up at rescues and shelters or are even euthanised simply because of incorrect breed selection by the owner. A little time spent in studying all of the various breed characteristics will save a great deal of heartache in the months and years ahead but where do you begin? There are numerous books on breeds, and the prospective puppy owner should first try to draw up a shortlist of breeds that he or she likes and then spend a few weeks of study at the local library to find out all of the desirable characteristics of each of the breeds in question.

Books written on individual breeds are usually written by people who are biased towards that breed. In order to get a balanced view it is a good idea to have a talk with one or two instructors at local dog-training clubs and your local vet; they will no doubt be able to relate any common, breed specific problems that they regularly encounter with your selected breed(s). What you obviously need to find out are all the good things and all of the bad things about the breed(s) you are interested in.

In Great Britain The Kennel Club will send you a list of breeders of any breed you specify if you write to them at , 1 Clarges St, Piccadilly, London. Alternatively, you can contact some of the leading breeders by purchasing one of the several dog periodicals and thumbing through the advertisements. How about the "Pets for Sale" column of your local newspaper?. Here you will need to exercise caution, because many 'casual' breeders will not know very much about the dogs they are breeding and may not be aware of the need for worming, vaccinations or registrations (where applicable). etc. You should also bear in mind that if you buy a puppy from such a source you will be very much on your own should problems start to occur, whereas a larger breeder has a reputation to protect and will be in a much better position to offer help and advice.

When you have located a litter of puppies of your chosen breed or better still two or three litters, make an appointment to go and see them and ask two simple questions. Ask if you may view the puppies with the mother present and also ask where the puppies are at the time that you are on the telephone. The dam is responsible for most of the learned behaviour patterns in her offspring, so a well-adjusted bitch is highly likely to produce puppies with a desirable temperament. If the breeder will not allow you to see mother and puppies together then suspect that mum's temperament is suspect. A common occurrence is for the bitch to show aggression when a stranger approaches her puppies. When the puppies witness this aggressive behaviour, it is highly probable that most will be influenced by it because of a process known as *observational learning*. This often results in the puppies exhibiting the condition known as nervous aggression as they grow and develop.

You should also be aware that if puppies are kept in an environment where they meet few people and have little in the way of stimulating and novel things to do then there is a risk of them lacking the skills necessary for good, social behaviour. Puppies raised in an enriched environment where they are often presented with new and novel things for them to explore are generally much easier to teach good social skills.

When you finally view a litter of puppies the rule is: Leave your money and cheque book at home! Sentiment will not then overrule common sense. It is all very well feeling sorry for the last puppy left in a litter, or the one cowering in the corner but remember that dogs do live for a long time and if you make a mistake in haste you may well learn to regret it at your leisure. I know that the majority of people when they go and view a litter will already have a mental picture of arriving back home with a 'new addition'. The children are excited, a collar, lead, basket, food bowls, etc., have already been purchased and everything is ready and waiting.

Nearly all breeders know that once someone arrives to view the pups, a sale is virtually guaranteed. Even if the person wants a dog and there are only bitches left, they *want* to be persuaded to take a bitch. They may even take a puppy of a different breed, as long as they go home with *something*. The golden rule is to never select a puppy unless you have seen at least two litters. The breeder may well pull the old "I have other people coming to see the puppies" routine but don't be fooled into making a quick decision by this. A reputable breeder who truly cares about the future welfare of the puppies that they breed will want to make sure that you are given enough time to enable you to make the right choice.

I wish there was a foolproof way of picking a puppy, but unfortunately there isn't. The best guide is to watch the puppies playing and eating; you will then get some idea as to which are the more dominant and which are more submissive. An experienced breeder may be able to advise you on individual temperaments within a litter. You will also get some idea of how quiet or active an individual is in relation to the rest of it's littermates. Pay a second visit a couple of days later so that you can compare this litter with any others that you have seen and will be able to judge if your assessment of 'character' remains unchanged. On the first visit a dog who seemed quiet may have been playing for an hour before you arrived, and on the second visit be the liveliest pup in the litter. It is, therefore, always advisable to delay making a decision unless you are certain that the puppy you pick is the right one. I have not mentioned appearance because that is a matter of personal preference. I would bet that an awful lot of people would be tempted to take home a tiger cub from the local zoo even logic should tell us that full-grown tigers do not make the best pets! It is pointless, therefore, my saying that you should pick the one that you like the look of.

The best age to acquire a puppy is between six and twelve weeks of age, while it is still dependent on its mother. Dogs purchased over sixteen weeks of age that have been kennelled with their mother or litter mates can prove extremely difficult to socialise correctly with people. It is for this reason that you want the puppy whilst it is still dependent on it's mother and therefore, able and willing to transfer this dependency to you.

Let us now assume that you have made your choice and handed over the money. The puppy is now your responsibility for the rest of its life. Whatever the breed, its ultimate development is down to you. Will it grow to become an obedience champion, perfect companion or will it be put to sleep before it is two years old for becoming aggressive ? You and not the puppy hold the answers to all of these questions.

Car Travel

Your pup's education begins with the journey home, and already most people have started making mistakes. Just suppose that we had a Saint Bernard pup and let it travel home on someone's lap on the front seat of the car. All of the way home the dog is continually stroked and petted to reassure it. It might be taken out, travelling in the same manner, to show it off to friends and relations or going to and from the vet's for vital inoculations. Then the decision is made that the dog is now too large, for comfort or safety, to remain on the front seat and a dog guard is purchased with the result that the dog barks and whines continually because he objects to being restricted to an area where he doesn't want to be; he may even learn to drag the dog guard down. To my way of thinking it is cruel for you to allow a dog to sit on your lap in the car and be petted, only to punish it at a later stage because it wants to do exactly what you have trained it to do! For the first and subsequent journeys it is just as easy to teach the pup to lie on or behind the back seat by placing it on a warm rug in a cardboard box, and this method will be more effective and cheaper than a dog guard. Start the way you mean to continue and you will reduce the chances of problems developing.

Feeding

The chances are that when you purchased your puppy you obtained a diet sheet from the breeder. If not, then any of the major dog-food manufacturers will happily advise you on your pup's daily nutritional requirements. In order to prevent the possibility of problems occurring at a later date, it is important that correct habits are instilled at an early age. First of all you should understand that your puppy must be taught that he does not have exclusive right to any food that you may choose to give him. If you allow him to growl at you whilst he is eating his food or a bone, are you also going to accept that when he is fully mature he also has the right to bite you to protect 'his' joint of meat that you have left defrosting on the work surface in the kitchen. Similarly, if you allow him to become protective over a bone as a puppy, do not be surprised if your dog attacks a child if it crawls towards him whilst he is eating.

The best way of avoiding the possibility of food aggression occurring in the first place is to feed the puppy out of three separate bowls, spaced evenly on the floor, each containing one third of the meal. This system allows you to regularly approach and lift one of the bowls and place something extra tasty on top of the food. In no time at all, because there is now no feeling of being deprived of a food bowl, any aggression present should decrease. If you only fed the puppy out of one bowl and tried to lift the bowl while the pup was eating it may well resent being deprived of the food. With three bowls, even if you lift one whilst the pup is eating, then there are two more available to him. Apply the same technique when giving chewsticks or marrowbones.

For more serious or persistent problems of food aggression with puppies it is advisable to first have the puppy checked over by a vet to make sure that there are no underlying medical problems that would cause the behaviour. In some instances simply shaking the puppy by the scruff of the neck, squirting water at him or tapping him on the nose with one finger may well achieve the desired result. If you have tried any of these methods and the aggression has dramatically increased as a result then contact your local trainer or behaviour consultant for advice.

It is also a good idea to ensure that *all* food is placed in his bowl for him to eat. If you allow him to take food from your hands when finishing a meal you will invariably end up with a dog that begs at the table for food. If, on the other hand, you have placed any left-over scraps in his bowl, he will be conditioned to wait by his bowl whilst you are eating your meal, leaving you in peace.

Your dog's mealtimes should, if possible, be planned to *follow* your own. An already dominant dog that is fed before the family sit down to eat is being told every day of his life that he is the most important member of the 'pack' because of the preferential treatment he receives at mealtimes.

Sleeping Areas

Where do you want your dog to sleep at night ?

Once again we need to look at the habits that we want to set for the rest of the dog's life and train it accordingly right from the start. Let us imagine that a young couple buy a German Shepherd puppy and decide that they don't mind if it sleeps in the bedroom. That arrangement is fine for two years until the imminent arrival of a new baby. The couple then decide that the bedroom is perhaps not the best place for the dog to sleep and relegate it to the kitchen. They then wonder why they get a behaviour change in their dog that they incorrectly define as jealousy.

Think very carefully indeed about allowing your dog to sleep on your bed, because of the risk of flea infestation. If your dog picks up one of these irritating parasites, as he almost certainly will at some time or another, you will not only have to kill all of the fleas on him but also the fleas and eggs that are on and in the covers of your bed. Fleas lay eggs on anything that the dog may lie on and when they hatch, they re-infest him.

In order to help you decide on an appropriate sleeping place at night, all of the common areas are listed together with advantages and disadvantages.

1. *Outside kennel:* This is fine for a long coated dog. Because the dog can adjust his coat dependent on the seasons of the year, moulting is reduced. The coat is therefore generally in a better condition than if the dog were kept inside. It is not, however, advisable to keep a short-coated dog overnight in a kennel in winter unless it is heated.

A dog kept in a kennel overnight is not able to deter burglars from gaining entry to the house but could warn of prowlers in the vicinity of the house by barking.

2. *In a basket/dog bed/indoor kennel in the kitchen:* This is a favourite sleeping place as the dog is usually not disturbed by traffic/people going past the front of the house. It is also well placed to give warning of the approach of an intruder to the territory, as many burglars attempt to gain entry by the kitchen door/window. However, remember what was said about possession of food earlier; if your dog growls over its food then it is foolhardy to allow the dog to sleep in the kitchen as it would almost certainly start guarding its territory from you ! It can also be dangerous to have a dog in the kitchen at all because of the possibility of tripping over it whilst carrying hot liquids, etc.

3. *In the lounge:* As the most expensive items in the house are usually kept in the lounge – TV, hi-fi, etc. – then the dog is arguably in the best position to defend these, but a dog that sheds it's coat profusely on the carpet/furniture can cause problems for the house proud owner. Even if you provide a basket for the dog to lie in he might find the armchair or settee more comfortable, so you might insist from day one that this is not acceptable or the furniture may eventually be used as a breeding ground for fleas! It is also unfair on the dog to allow it to get up on the furniture one day, but scold it when it climbs up with wet or muddy feet another day.

4. *Hall, stairs and landing:* The dog is now well placed to defend the territory, but might be encouraged to bark at everything that passes by the front of the house. It may also be difficult to position the bed or basket where you are not constantly tripping over it. Behaviour problems such as guarding food preparation areas, furniture and sleeping area are greatly minimised, and if the hall is cooler than the rest of the house then the dog's coat will improve. You will also eliminate most of the unwanted hair from the furniture.

5. *Bedroom:* A lot of people feel secure if the dog sleeps in the bedroom because if anyone breaks in, the dog is in the best place to defend them . . . Rubbish. Just look at it logically. Right from the beginning although you may encourage the dog to bark if anyone comes to the front or back door, you will positively discourage the act of barking when anyone actually enters the house, otherwise the dog becomes a nuisance and even a liability.

So the dog learns that, whilst it is all right to bark and show aggression to anyone on the outside of the house, he must under no circumstances show any aggression once that person enters but must accept them. It follows then that the dog is more effective in *preventing* anyone gaining entry. I get many telephone calls every year from owners who have lost most of their precious posessions whilst they and their dog were fast asleep upstairs!

Unless your dog is particularly dominant it should accept anyone entering your bedroom at any time of the day or night.

If, however, we have certain types of behaviour problems when we leave the dog by itself, such as chewing, or house training, then the bedroom may be the best place for the dog to sleep.

Something else to bear in mind is that when I mentioned sleeping areas, I am also referring to an area where the dog can be left when the rest of the family need to go out. If we teach the dog to sleep in the bedroom at night but every time we go out we lock him up in the kitchen, we shouldn't be surprised if he objects!

What's in a name?

A great deal of confusion often arises when it comes to the naming of a puppy. The fact is that the vast majority of pet dogs simply do not know their own names! Take the case of a Boxer called Rocky.

Dad comes in from work and calls the dog over to greet him: " Hello Rock, what have you been up to today?" The youngest child then comes in and greets the dog by saying "Come on Rocket, let's go into the garden and play with the ball". The eldest child comes in and says, "Fetch your lead, Sprocket, and I'll take you for a walk". Mum on the other hand, particularly when she is in a good mood, always refers to him as Muttley. Out in the park after the exercise has finished Dad calls him back to put him on the lead: "Here Rock, good boy." "Rock" ignores this. Now he is in trouble, and the command "Rocky come here" is given in a really stern voice. After being left at home whilst the family are out shopping for an hour, they return to find the edge of the carpet has been chewed. "Rocky, who's done this?" Mum growls.

So which name does the dog think applies to him? Rocky, Rock, Sprocket or Muttley. If you think that's confusing for the dog, wait and see what happens when they all try to 'train' the dog to understand some basic commands. Imagine going to the local dog-training club and the instructor saying "Use the dogs name and the command 'heel' ". If Dad says "Rocky heel", the dog will immediately think that he is in trouble because as part of his everyday life he only hears the name Rocky when he is about to be chastised. The average pet owner can substitute the word 'confused' for the word 'defiant' in their vocabulary when talking about their dog's behaviour. This is a much more accurate description of situations that develop where the dog supposedly "stands and defies me".

All names are best kept to just one or two syllables. However, as most single syllable names are capable of being lengthened by the addition of the letter y or ie, and two syllable words shortened, when you choose a name everyone should be told only ever to use the name in it's original form, each and every time they speak to the dog. By doing this the dog will learn that when he hears his name someone is specifically referring to him, which will then gain his attention. The word that follows the name, together with the owners facial expression, will tell him either the response that is required or whether he has been a good or a bad boy.

Games and Education

A dog's behaviour in later life is influenced by the games he plays as a puppy. This factor is almost always overlooked by the dogs owner, trainers and so called behaviourists alike, and yet is one of the most fundamental observations of all animal (and human) behaviour. If I allow a puppy to bite my fingers, and if he learns, during this game, that he can get me to react and withdraw my hand by applying slightly more pressure with his teeth, when he is six months old should I be surprised if he uses the 'game' to remove my hand that is trying to comb away the tangles behind his ears? If I play tug-of-war games with a rubber ring and encourage him to growl at me and eventually let him win the game by allowing him to take the rubber ring off me, should I be surprised that at a year old he has learnt that in games of strength that involve possession he can beat me every time?

In bringing up a puppy, the transition from birth to maturity can be influenced not only in games it plays, but also by its interpretation of any rules that exist. During the upbringing phase we must educate our puppy through the games that we allow it to play and make use of its natural instincts and abilities. If I had a child that I caught in the act of dismantling the television with a screwdriver he had stolen from my tool chest, I would probably buy him a Meccano set and his own screwdriver. That way I could encourage him to develop manual dexterity and creativity and give him an outlet for his enquiring mind. If I tried to suppress his natural talent by smacking him he might well never touch the television again, but turn his attention to the hi-fi!.

Fight against the natural instinct by trying to mechanically or mentally 'block' it and it is sure to resurface in another way. Stop a dog chasing bicycles and it will start chasing joggers. Stop it chasing joggers and it may turn it's attention to livestock. Our education process should take into account not only what we expect from the dog but also what the dog expects from us and from life. So what are the fundamental things we need to teach our dogs? This, of course, will depend partly on the reasons for acquiring a dog in the first place. A dog that is to be trained to work in obedience competitions is going to be taught a different set of 'games' and rules from a dog which is to be kept as a pet and companion for a family.

This aside, there are still some basic educational requirements, most of which will apply to both pet and competition dogs.

1. To accept every person in the household (pack) as being more dominant. (To respect authority).
2. To feel secure in both its environment and in the company of its owners (pack).
3. To trust; learn how take and give affection.
4. To be socially acceptable to the local community and environment. This includes mixing with other dogs.
5. To develop an individual character which fits in with the life style and habits of the household (pack).
6. To be allowed to develop skills and instincts to the advantage of the household (pack).
7. To be attached to and influenced by the human family members but also to be independent enough not to resent being detached from them for short periods.

We could just as easily be talking about a young child as a young dog, couldn't we?

So what sorts of educational games can we play to achieve these requirements? Let's deal with them in sequence.

1. *Dominance:* A lot of people are under the mistaken impression that dominance involves the use of physical force. It doesn't have to. I play a game of tug-of-war but always end up ultimately winning possession of the rubber ring and putting it away where the dog cannot gain access to it until

I choose to invite him to play with it when *I* want to, then I have taught him a). that I am physically superior and can always beat him in strength and possession games and b). for behaviour that I want to encourage he can win a game with *my* toy. I can place the ring on the floor whilst he is asleep and then, when he wakes and moves towards it, I can snatch it from under his nose and put it away. When he is resting in his basket or on his rug, I can move him and sit there myself on odd occasions. Whenever I feed him, I can mix up his food and not let him touch it until I have eaten a biscuit. If he picks up articles that I do not want him to have and he runs away with them inviting me to chase him, I attach a fine line to his collar and leave things lying around for him to steal and then when he does so I gently pull him towards me, take the article from him and replace it, inviting him to steal again. He will soon learn that games of chase and possession are never won and he will accept that I am in control. If you already own a dog and these games sound familiar could it be because your own dog is now controlling you because it has taught you the rules of these dominance games (see 'Behaviour Groups' page 36). If everyone in the household plays these games observing the same set of rules they all remain above him in the pack order.

2. *Security:* You must give your puppy a regular feed time and provide him with a safe environment. You can also teach him to accept anyone who is invited in by letting them feed him or play with one of his owner's (pack leader's) toys. If visiting children come round you must ensure that their advances towards the dog and any subsequent games do not become overpowering or oppressive.

When first taken into the big outside world the puppy can carry a favourite toy to make the environment a pleasant experience. If another dog threatens you should chase it away, thereby ensuring that the puppy gains the maximum amount of confidence and security within its family. He will also understand, in times of stress, that his pack will take care of him. Allowing people to feed him when out on walks can also be beneficial in developing good social behaviour.

3. *Trust and affection:* When we talk about affection we generally mean touching and stroking. If the puppy gets stroked and fussed twenty-four hours a day he comes to regard this as a take-it-or-leave-it function. He then starts to 'demand' attention when *he* wants it and learns all sorts of attention-seeking behaviour by trial-and-error approach.

A friend comes in and he barks constantly for attention because no one is taking any notice of him. On the other hand, take him out for exercise and he runs off because there are more interesting things around than his owner. Lying by the fire, you walk over and try to stroke him and he gets up and walks away. The whole point about affection is that it has to be earned. If the pup does something that pleases you then show him affection. If you do something that pleases the pup, allow him to give you some affection. If the puppy comes up to you whilst you are occupied doing something and wants to be made a fuss of, make him do something such as sit, lie down, fetch, etc., to earn your affection otherwise you will reduce your pup's desire to work to please you.If you observe the rules of the game you can then teach your pup to obey commands *when he is most receptive to learning*, ie, when he comes up and wants to do something to win your affection.

4. *Social acceptability:* Barking when left alone is a frequent cause of annoyance to neighbours and it is well worth the effort, with a young puppy, to teach him to spend some time on his own in one room of the house whilst you watch television for an hour or so. It is never a good plan to allow any dog to follow you around the house for twenty-four hours a day. If the pup cannot learn to remain in a room by himself when you are just the other side of the door in the next room then you have no chance of being able to leave the pup alone in the house for any length of time without problems developing. *Any* barking between six weeks and six months of age should be strictly controlled by the owner. I would verbally reprimand any young puppy if it barked at visitors to the house, people outside the house, or other dogs. Barking for attention is arguably the worst form of annoyance both for the owners and neighbours and should be discour-

aged from the beginning. As the dog starts to approach maturity we can **teach** him to bark under certain circumstances if necessary. He will then only bark if the training conditions are met and will not bark indiscriminately. This training can take any form such as protection of owner or territory or only when a specific command is given.

I hope that it goes without saying that we should take steps to ensure that our puppy doesn't foul pavements, playgrounds or children's play areas. A routine must be established whereby the pup starts to learn by habit that there are certain areas where fouling is acceptable (see 'house-training', page 58). The puppy should only be exercised in areas where he will not cause annoyance to the local community. It is a good plan to go and find one or two areas for exercise before even contemplating the purchase of a puppy, as a lack of suitable exercise facilities may well influence the choice of breeds.

The correct social behaviour towards other dogs and people should be taught at every opportunity that presents itself early in the pup's life. A child may well be equally afraid of a 'friendly' pup that jumps up and knocks it over, as it is of a puppy that stands off and barks and growls.

5. *Character development:* Having got the puppy home the most important thing is that the pup should learn and adapt to and fit in with the owner's life style. This takes place at the outset because the daily routines that take place must be aimed at the way the dog is required to behave later in life. If you have a circle of friends and lead an active social life, don't change your life just because you have a new puppy. Even before the pup is fully inoculated, you can still take him for car trips, or carry him in your arms to visit neighbours and socialise him with people. If you want your puppy to be friendly with people, it is no good putting him into solitary confinement for six weeks and then expecting not to have problems. Imagine putting a three-year old child in solitary confinement until it is five and then expecting it to go to school without any problems and to be receptive to learning.

We should also encourage friends to play games with the

puppy and always see that the games never get out of hand. During early life we can allow him to develop his individual character by being neither too overpowering nor too easy-going. Consistency is the name of the game.

6. *Skills and creativity:* If I have a puppy that enjoys chasing a ball, by carefully channelling that instinct I can teach him to find a 'lost' ball using his sense of smell, and retrieve it. I can then teach him a game of 'hunt the thimble' (only using the ball). I can invite the children to hide the ball in a room (or outside the house) and send the dog to find and retrieve. This game will occupy him mentally and physically and will also make the dog a favourite with visiting children as well as my own!

How about the dog that enjoys carrying things around in its mouth? If I buy that dog its own shopping basket, I can make use of this behaviour by teaching it to carry its own food back from the shops.

If the dog has a good sense of smell I can teach it a game of find the lady. Using three playing cards, a friend handles two and I place a third card (Queen) face down. A dog can be trained to easily find and retrieve the one which bears my scent!

In short, if I give my dog all the interest and games he needs within the needs of the family, he will not go out seeking adventures and mischief of his own. Whatever the puppy does, try and modify its actions into something that you will find acceptable or even useful in later life. If your puppy shows an aptitude for opening doors, teach him how to close them after him. If he greets you when you get in from work by picking something up in his mouth and bringing it to you, leave your slippers near the door and encourage him to bring these to you. You can progressively move the slippers further away and only take any notice of him for specially fetching the slippers. Ignore him for fetching anything else. So you see we haven't stopped a natural desire we have merely encouraged a behaviour to develop into an area of benefit to us.

Toys

Most dogs have lots of toys. Unfortunately, unless used correctly more behaviour problems are due to incorrect use of toys than any other single factor. We can divide toys into three main groups as follows:

1. *Chasing toys.* Ball, Frisbee, Kong, etc. These exploit the dog's natural desire to chase after moving prey. The fact that the dog may not pick the thrown article up and return with it is immaterial as long as it wants to chase after the toy when it is thrown.
2. *Killing toys.* Squeaky toys, rag to shake etc. These toys exploit a dog's killing instinct and the dog will bite and shake the toy, sometimes in an extremely excitable way, and lose interest after it is 'dead', ie., the squeaker stops working.
3. *Possession toys.* Rubber ring, pull rope, etc. The dog uses these to play games of strength, dominance and possession, usually 'inviting' the owner to play and then growling in the attempt to assert his supremacy over whoever he is pulling against.

It can sometimes be a little confusing that some dogs may enjoy **chasing** a rubber ring and not use it for possession at all! An old slipper may be used by the dog to satisfy any of the above instincts.

Whichever toy your dog prefers the important thing is that you must teach him that they are **your** toys which he can win a game with for the right behaviour. Let him think that *he* either owns the toys or is allowed to set the rules under which he plays and he will invariably use these toys to teach **you** the behaviours that *he* wants. Let us take each of the groups of toys and see what behaviour we are likely to get if we fail to control games.

Chase toys: The games start with the dog chasing a toy, such as a ball. He may then decide to chase the person's hand holding his ball, and then the ball that next door's children are playing with. The ball game in the local park attracts his attention, and he assumes that he has the exclusive right to chase everything that resembles a ball. If a child picks up the ball and runs he will chase the child, etc.

If we teach the dog right from the start that it isn't **his** ball and he is only 'invited' to play if **we** want a game, two things happen: he will be keen to work to please us to win a game with the ball; he never learns to chase anything and everything – only what we want him to chase.

Killing toys: Let him have unsupervised access to killing toys and he will chew them, mimicking the act of killing by biting, tearing and shaking. When his toys are destroyed he may well attack carpets, soft furnishings, his cushions, etc. Although the poor owner will attempt to teach his dog to be more selective in the items he chews, the dog has assumed that everything is his to chew by right. It is no good giving a dog an old slipper to chew and then expecting it to differentiate between that and an expensive pair of shoes.

Possessions toys: Potentially the most dangerous category of all toys to allow the dog to 'own', and the single biggest cause of dogs attacking their owners. If you leave any possession toys lying around for the dog to play with he may then protect his toy and the area where he puts the toy. He may also start possessing other items that he thinks belong to him and other areas of the house, namely furniture, beds and food preparation areas.

None of my dogs own toys and yet I play with my own dogs with toys more than most other dog owners ever would. The difference is that I allow my dogs to play **with me** with **my toys**. That is I am using my toys to communicate with my dogs. At the end of each 'game' with whichever toy the dog and I are playing with, the toy is put away where the dog has no access to it.

In case you think that your dog needs to be left with a selection of toys to amuse himself with when you go out and leave him alone, he doesn't. A good marrowbone or reconstituted rawhide chew should suffice to relieve boredom. Dogs seldom, if ever, play with toys in isolation unless it is a game of destruction. It is far better to leave a large marrowbone for the puppy to gnaw whilst you are out. When you return, pick it up and keep it in an old biscuit tin; that way the dog will not get bored with it. A tip here is to fasten a piece of string around the centre of the bone and tie the other end near the dog's sleeping area. He will not then be able to carry it around and put it on any furniture.

Children and Puppies

Puppies should never be purchased as toys for children to play with for basically the same reasons as I wouldn't give a puppy a toy to *own*. A child under the age of seven should only be allowed supervised access to a puppy or even an adult dog for that matter. If I am not there to educate both the pup and the child as to one another's requirements then games get completely out of hand to the point where the dog or child suffer either mental or physical discomfort. I would want to teach the child how to look after and care for the pup, the games that are acceptable and the ones that are not. I would also want to teach the pup to accept the child as being superior and to teach it the rules of any acceptable games. We can also use the dog's upbringing for educational purposes and teach a relationship based on trust and understanding. The thing that we must prevent is the child seeing the puppy as something which it may discard, at will, should the novelty wear off, in the same way that a toy is discarded two weeks after Christmas. No contact at all is better than unsupervised contact.

Housetraining

Providing the mother of the pup has encouraged the right type of behaviour and the environment during the first weeks of life with the breeder has allowed the pup to leave the 'nest' to relieve itself, housetraining should be a relatively easy process.

We can start by ensuring that he is taken to the spot where we want him to perform immediately after feeding him and immediately after waking up. At these times he will be most likely to want to relieve himself and we can take advantage of this fact in order to help in our housetraining programme.

It is a good idea to reserve a small part of the garden for the dog to use. If he has an accident in the house while you are there, you can only reprimand him *if you catch him in the act*.

It is then usually sufficient to growl and give him a quick shake by the scruff of the neck. If he has finished by the time you get to him, omit the shake! The puddle or parcel that the pup has deposited on the floor must now be removed and placed outside in the area where we want him to go. If it is a puddle, you can place a couple of sheets of newspaper down to absorb it and place these in the garden on your chosen spot weighting them down with a few stones. The next time you take him out to relieve himself, take him to the spot and let him sniff. As soon as he performs, make a great fuss of him, have a quick game with his favourite toy before taking him back into the house. The wrong way to go about housetraining is to smack the dog *after* it has had an accident and/or to put it into the garden unsupervised.

The chances are that if you do this, the dog's attention will simply be focused on getting back into the house. You must accompany the pup in order to educate it. At first the visits outside will be made at random intervals, dictated mainly by the sleep/eating/drinking patterns of the pup. Slowly, however, habits will form so that the pup's body clock will be regulated to perform natural functions at specific times, these times being dictated by set feed times, exercise times, and the sleeping and waking hours of its owner.

How about during the night? Most puppies are incapable of lasting as much as eight hours, so we must guard against the floor being soiled, otherwise the pup will use its nose to locate its 'toilet' night after night. The easiest way is to put a polythene sheet on the floor and then put two or three sheets of newspaper on top of it. The polythene, which needs to be slightly bigger than the size of the newspaper, will prevent the floor beneath from absorbing the smell. The newspaper should be placed near the door of the room where the puppy is, and its bed should be positioned as far away from the newspaper as possible. Most pups will learn to relieve themselves as far away from their 'nest' as possible before they are four weeks old, but there are occasions when this may not happen (see 'House cleanliness', page 58), due to the environment they were kept in as pups. It would help if the top sheet of the newspaper could be dabbed in a spot of the pup's urine so that he can use his nose to locate the papers in the dark. Once the pup learns to use the paper during the night, as he gets older you can move the paper, in stages, under the door until it eventually ends up outside the door. Then at any time that the pup wants to answer the call of nature he will go to the door and stand (possibly crying) waiting to be let out and will 'hold on' until he is let out to his spot in the garden. You can now possibly see that the area where the dog sleeps may have a bearing on successful housetraining. But what if you have tried house-training the pup for several weeks to no avail? The chapter on behaviour lists all of the problems on housetraining and gives advise on cures.

A day in the life of a puppy

Let us look at the typical daily routine assuming that the pup is owned by an 'average' family.

7a.m. Dad gets up and greets the puppy, clearing away any soiled newspapers and takes pup out to his spot in the garden, waiting with him to reward him by playing with a toy when he has performed. After a few minutes' play the pup is brought back into the house and left alone whilst breakfast is prepared. As each member of the family comes downstairs to greet him he runs up and is taught to sit before anyone makes a fuss of him. Whilst the family sit down for breakfast, the pup is actively discouraged from crying at the table for food either by ignoring him completely or by growl-ing *no* at him. As soon as breakfast is finished the pup is given his first meal of the day and taught to obey the com-mand 'come' when calling him towards the food bowl. As soon as the meal is over the children can take the pup out into the garden. If and when he relieves himself, a game can be played with a favourite toy but all of the game is observed by Mum and Dad who will discourage games where the pup gets over excited or games that involve the puppy jumping up or using his teeth on anything other than the toy. At the completion of the exercise session the toys are put away, the kids go off to school and Dad goes to work. Mum has to go to the local shops and so puts the pup into the back of the car on its own blanket. Because it is not fully inoculated she cannot get it out of the car near the shops and so gives it a marrowbone to amuse itself with whilst she does the shopping.

As soon as she returns home the pup is taken to its spot in the garden and a ten minute play session follows with toys. At the completion of the games the toys are put away and the pup is allowed to roam about at will but is discouraged from going upstairs. If someone comes to the door and the pup barks, it will be actively discouraged and the person standing on the other side of the door is invited in and asked to spend a few seconds playing with one of the toys to teach the puppy to accept and enjoy the company of everyone that is invited into the house.

The lunch time meal is omitted because the pup is due for his first injection at the vet's at 1.00pm and so a few tasty pieces of liver are placed in a margarine tub prior to putting the pup in the back of the car. At the vet's surgery, the receptionist is told that the pup is due for its injections but has been left in the back of the car until it is time to see the vet. There is no point in sitting in a waiting room with the puppy where there is a possibility of picking up infection from other patients who may be 'off colour' and waiting to see the vet. When the time comes the pup is taken in, fondled and examined by the vet. As the pup is now ravenous as he has missed lunch, the margarine tub of liver is produced and just before the injection is given the tub is placed near the pup and it is allowed to eat. A final fuss is made by the vet and the pup is carried out and put back in the car.

On the way home Mum calls in at the pet shop and buys a soft collar and lead and takes it to try on the pup for size back in the car. She then drives back home, lifts the puppy out of the car and takes him into the garden. A fifteen minute play session follows after the pup has relieved itself.

The pup is now fairly tired, and on entering the house flops down under the chair in the living room to sleep.

Mum picks him up and puts him in his bed in the kitchen. When the pup wakes up, later on, he is immediately taken out into the garden. After ten minutes of accompanied exercise he is brought back into the house and the collar is placed loosely around his neck and the toys brought out for a game for ten minutes. During the game, he only pauses for a few seconds to scratch at the collar because his mind is fully occupied with chasing the ball across the floor. The pup doesn't actually bring the ball back yet but prefers to take it under the coffee table at the far end of the room where the game is taking place.

At that point the children come home from school and call the puppy to them adding the command 'come' after his name. Both children are careful to make the pup sit before fussing him, and any attempt to jump up is firmly discouraged. A toy is taken out of the cupboard and one child holds the pup whilst the other first excites him with the toy, and then hides it behind the magazine rack. The pup is then released with the words 'find'. On the first two occasions the pup is successful and soon loses interest but, with a little help and encouragement, he quickly cottons on to where the toy is hidden and picks it up, running under the coffee table with it to lie down and chew it. Each time this happens the toy is recovered and eventually, when the puppy begins to tire of the game, the toy is put back into the cupboard out of the pup's way. Dad then comes in and calls the pup to him adding the command 'come'. As before, jumping up is firmly discouraged, but whilst he is stroking the pup it starts to 'play bite' his fingers in excitement. The correction is firm and immediate. The pup is given a sharp tap across the nose with the fingers he is biting and hears the growled command *'no!'* which makes him jump back in surprise. Dad immediately encourages him to come back and continues to stroke and pet him. The game of finger biting is not a pleasant game for him to play so the pup does not repeat this behaviour.

The family then sit down for a meal and discourage the pup from crying for food. As soon as the meal is finished the pup is called to the kitchen adding the command *'come'* to his name, and his food is placed down for him only when he has obeyed the command *'sit'* by holding the food up and pushing his bottom to the floor. During his meal one of the children, supervised by Dad, goes up to gently stroke him for a few seconds. The pup's only reaction is to continue eating but wag his tail. Dad then takes him out into the garden for ten minutes. Unfortunately, it is now raining and so when they come back in the house the pup is towelled dry. During this drying session the pup starts to wriggle and turn it into a game by biting and pulling at the towel. The command *'no!'* is repeated in a growled voice, and he is physically held until he stands still and accepts the towel without trying to play with it ... The rest of the drying process takes place without incident and at the finish the pup stands, wagging his tail. He is then quickly brushed and his paws are picked up and examined. In order to accustom him to being handled, his ears, teeth, gums and under his tail are all quickly checked. By now the pup is starting to tire, and after a few minutes of wandering around he flops down beside the coffee table. As soon as this happens he is picked up and placed in his bed in the kitchen and the door is closed. The family then sit down to watch the television.

After about an hour and a half mum goes into the kitchen to make a cup of tea and the puppy wakes up. One of the children 'volunteered' to take the pup into the garden to its spot.

When everyone has finished their tea the pup is allowed to come into the lounge for a game with a toy. Once again, each time that the pup picks the toy up he takes it under the coffee table. Dad then decides to teach the pup to take it to him on the command come. To do this he throws the toy across the room and, whilst the pup is running out to pick it up, moves from where he was sitting to just in front of the coffee table. Sure enough the pup brings the toy to him! A great fuss is made of him and the toy is thrown several times more and each time he picks it up he runs

directly back to the coffee table where dad is waiting to make
a fuss of him.

After the game the toy is put away in the cupboard. The
new collar is then placed on for twenty minutes and then
removed. The pup is offered a light meal just as the children
are going to bed and is then taken into the garden.

On returning inside the pup's paws are dried without any
problems. Later that night he is taken out one final time
and newspapers are placed in the polythene sheet by the
back door, the pup is placed in his bed and another day is
over.

So what has the pup learnt? The answer is an awful lot,
but the important thing is that he has started to learn both
acceptable and unacceptable behaviour. On top of that he
is also being allowed an outlet for his natural instincts and
he is also learning to be creative. Briefly, we can sum up the
learning as follows:

Pleasant Experiences	*Unpleasant Experiences*
Travelling in the car	Biting fingers
Going to the vet's	Biting the towel
Games with the owner's toys	Crying for food
Feed times	Barking
Exercise in the garden	
Family returning to house	
Being stroked	
Going to bed in the kitchen	
Hide-and-seek with toys	

The pup is also starting to *want* to obey the commands
'*come*', '*sit*' and '*find*' and is continuing to learn his name.
There is a good chance that he will want to repeat all of the
pleasant experiences later in life and not to repeat all of the
unpleasant experiences, or specifically the actions that lead
up to the unpleasant experiences. It is also a tremendous
advantage if the pup learns to be handled without resentment. Just imagine the dog getting an ear infection later in
life that needs urgent treatment, but not letting the owner
put in the drops prescribed by the vet!

Of course, the story about the puppy doesn't take into account the 'what ifs'. For instance, what if the pup is play biting someone's fingers and the tap on the nose does not have any effect? You could try dipping your fingers into one of the many taste deterrents that are available. This often has the effect of decreasing the biting behaviour as your fingers now taste very unpleasant.

On the subject of corrective measures, you have to use a little common sense. The idea is never to cause physical pain of any sort, just simply a quick shock that is over in the twinkling of an eye. Repeatedly shaking a pup does nothing to foster the relationship between dog and owner. Some very submissive dogs respond simply to being growled at with any other form of correction being unnecessary. This is where an understanding of your individual dog comes in.

The prolonged use of verbal or physical corrections often results in a dog becoming desensitised to their effect with the result that you have to get firmer and firmer until correction becomes abuse.

2

Behaviour

Before any training is attempted, consideration should be given to learning as much as possible about canine behaviour. Most of the very successful competitive trainers have built up a wealth of knowledge of this subject, enabling them to work in harmony with their dogs, understanding and interpreting the varying patterns of behaviour; encouraging and channelling the behaviour required for domestic and competitive requirements and suppressing the socially unacceptable areas of behaviour.

In my own experience, there are three main categories of behaviour patterns and the majority of dogs will fall into any one of these areas, although it should be noted that some will fall midway between the lines that divide one area from another. Before looking at these groups, we should first look at the factors effecting behaviour from conception to maturity.

Ancestry

It is almost inevitable that, when discussing parentage, someone will come up with the often quoted expression, 'My dog has a pedigree as long as your arm'. So let us have a look at pedigrees and what information can be gained from them to give us some clues into possible behaviour.

I should start by saying that approximately one quarter of the pedigrees that I have been shown by owners of pedigree dogs have proved to be inaccurate, with some dogs on the pedigree forms being credited with fictitious qualifications, or well known stud dogs having wrong parentage. I have even seen pedigrees which do not bear any relationship to the breed of dog to which they are supposed to relate.

The first thing to look for in a pedigree is the qualifications obtained by any of the parents or grandparents (a list of commonly used abbreviations appears at the end of the book), to give us a clue as to the type of behaviour we are most likely to get.

A pedigree with dogs having predominantly breed qualifications i.e. SH.CH (show Champion) or CH (again meaning show champion), would tend to suggest that importance has primarily been placed by the breeders on the dog's physical attributes, chest, set of ears and tail, coat etc., with temperament, working potential and the basic instincts which place the dogs into different breed classifications being only of secondary importance.

A pedigree with predominantly working qualifications such as FT.CH (Field trials Champion) or W.T.Ch (Working trials Champion), will generally mean that the dog has been bred primarily for temperament, instinctive behaviour and working potential – if by chance or design dogs are produced that also conform to the various breed standards, this is a bonus, but of secondary importance.

A pedigree without any dogs being listed as having any qualifications will generally mean that no planned breeding regime has been carried out, which makes it more difficult to know if the dog will look like the breed it is supposed to represent when mature, or if it will carry the instincts and general temperament of its breed.

A mixture of working and breed qualifications does not necessarily mean good looks coupled with working instincts and ability; it could be exactly the opposite!

It might appear that a dog with predominantly working ancestry will be easier to train than a dog bred solely for looks. This unfortunately is far from the case, as a dog bred for work and kept purely as a pet will invariably be denied instinctive behaviour patterns and mental awareness and agility.

If you require a comfortable family saloon car capable of getting you from A to B with varying payloads and capable of pulling a caravan twice a year, you would hardly buy a high-powered sports car! So it is with dogs. If you are prepared to devote time and patience in exercising both body and mind, then a working pedigree may be the wisest choice.

Sire and Dam: This is the most important aspect of a dog's pedigree because, in terms of behaviour, a great many clues may be derived from a study of Mum and Dad.

Let us look at the sire first. Most reputable breeders will want to use the best available dog on their bitches, and so either the sire or the grandsire on the father's side will have some reason for being used at stud by way of qualifications. If the sire is fairly well known then contact may be made with other owners of his offspring to get some idea of the type and temperament of his progeny. Ideally, I would like to see and study the stud dog on several occasions to build up an idea of his temperament and to look for signs of undesireable behaviour such as aggression towards other dogs or people.

The dam is the most important parent as she is responsible for most of the behaviour patterns occurring in her offspring – not due to the genetic code, but due to the fact that she is responsible for formally instilling some measure of discipline within the litter, and also teaching her puppies various skills that will equip them for later life.

Nervousness is, in my experience, learnt from the dam rather than inherited from either parent. I have often seen nervous puppies from nervous bitches mated to really bold dogs, but have yet to find nervous puppies from a really bold, friendly bitch mated to a really nervous dog.

A lot of behaviour problems in a dog can be traced back to its mother. A sensible, well adjusted bitch will tend to produce sensible offspring, whilst a bitch that is aggressive with people will tend to teach her puppies this behaviour.

Behaviour Groups

Although we have talked briefly about ancestral reasons for particular traits, by far the biggest influence affecting behaviour is caused by the owners when the puppy is from four to sixteen weeks of age. Almost every problem directly accountable to the owner can be traced back to the important phase of development.

The development of an individual dog taken from a litter of puppies is dependant on the owners having an understanding of the dog's requirements, just as much as having a measure of control and discipline. No matter how well bred or costly a puppy is, a potential champion can end up having to be destroyed due to problems created entirely by the ignorance of its owner in understanding the dog.

The manner in which a dog is kept and its immediate environment is also a factor in setting behaviour traits. A dog brought up to reach maturity in isolation from other dogs may never learn to respond socially when confronted by a dog or dogs in any normal situation. I have know of several cases where one dog has been attacked by another because, although wanting to play, the wrong set of signals had been conveyed. Similarly, a dog brought up in a bungalow might easily panic the first time it is required to walk down a flight of stairs.

Behaviour groups can be divided into three as follows:

1. *Submissive.* At between four and ten weeks it becomes noticeable that although the puppy is willing to come when called and enjoys being stroked, it will either half close its eyes when looking at its owner, or turn its head slightly to avert his gaze so as to give very little eye contact. From about nine weeks to about six months or more when its owner returns home after being at work all day, the pup will run to greet him and will pass a few drops (sometimes more) of urine on the floor whilst being stroked. From about twelve weeks of age when the owner raises his/her voice in anger, the puppy will roll onto its back presenting its tummy in the classic submissive pose. This is occasionally followed at around twenty weeks by the puppy being unwilling to eat its meals in view of the owners; it will wait to be left alone before doing so.

With this type of dog, the control that the handler has is usually excellent and the dog will usually appear to be devoted. Although it may sound confusing, the dog that is submissive with people may sometimes be very dominant with the dogs it associates with.

Any form of compulsion, particularly during the first sixteen weeks, would tend to make the dog very subdued.

2. *Nervous.* This in my opinion, is started off by the mother. She will teach the puppies to distrust any person approaching by barking and raising her hackles.

From this point there is a vicious circle which is quite difficult to break. The puppy starts to learn that whenever anything threatens its home, owner or itself, it can get the desired reaction and get rid of the intruder by adopting a threatening attitude. This usually entails explosive barking and sometimes even making contact by snapping at the offending person or dog.

In actual fact, the dog exhibiting the symptoms of nervous aggression only becomes dangerous when, in a confined area simply because its main aim is to avoid confrontation even if, to do this, it sometimes needs to use its teeth.

To make matters worse, as the owner starts to become aware of the fact that, in certain circumstances, the dog will react in an aggressive manner, they tend to become over anxious of developing situations, causing the dog to react to their own nervousness.

The most common example of this generally starts to manifest itself at around the age of seven months when the dog, whilst walking with its owner, sees either a person or another dog approaching. The owner, aware of the possibility of aggression ocurring, begins to tighten the lead, and maybe also tries to give some verbal distraction. In fact, the only result is to increase the dog's awareness that its handler is apprehensive and it may then start to react by barking and showing aggression towards anyone in the immediate vicinity.

This type of dog also tends to be ever alert and usually almost obsessively bonded and devoted to its owners and the immediate family.

Submission and nervousness are often confused. They are not the same. A dog may be dominant and nervous or submissive but friendly.

3. *Dominant.* The single biggest problem facing a dog owner is whether or not his dog is going to be one of the relatively small percentage of dogs that grow up showing signs of dominant, out of control behaviour. With correct upbringing, even the most dominant of dogs can prove to be excellent family pets and/or working dogs. The development of dominant behaviour starts at a very early age and follows a fairly standard pattern. At four to six weeks, whilst still with its brothers and sisters, the puppy will start to bully the other puppies during play and sometimes during meal times. Its mother during this time will try to keep the puppy firmly in its place. If she has a large litter to look after then her job is made even more difficult. The puppy will usually move into its permanent home with new owners at around seven weeks of age. During meal times the puppy may demonstrate his trick of growling when anyone goes near his bowl which, of course, everyone thinks it's humorous and nobody does anything to stop. At various times through the day the pup wants to play and does so with great enthusiasm. Tug-of-war games are its favourite, and the owners start to develop scratches on their hands and fingers where the pup has started to mouth and bite. Toys are provided by the thoughtful owners which the pup has free access to, and which he will take to his owners when he wants to play.

At around twelve to fourteen weeks the rapidly growing pup may have started to snap when anyone approaches his food dish at meal times, although he has not actually bitten. During the play sessions, the dog will insist that the handler keeps on with the game until the dog decides he has had enough. Toys, particularly tug-of-war toys, are kept in or around the place where the dog sleeps. If at this stage the dog thinks a slipper or shoe or handbag, etc. would make a nice toy he will steal it, and when the owners try to take it from the pup he will run away, usually under or behind obstacles such as a sideboard. when the owner puts his hand under, the puppy again demonstrates his ability to keep its owner away by growling/snapping.

At around six months the young dog decides that the armchair makes a better bed than his plastic basket and any attempts to get him off result in growling/snapping. During games of tug-of-war the dog now always wins by showing aggression to gain possession and, when it does so, retires to its place of rest to deposit its bounty. If the owner enjoys wrestling games with the dog on the floor, at various times the dog will push its chin across the back of the handler's neck and shoulders.

Approaching maturity, the dog now has a chair or settee of its own near to which its toys are kept. If the owners try to move the dog when it is resting or attempt to take anything from the dog that it may be guarding, they get bitten for their efforts.

At various times when the family are preparing themselves a meal, the dog starts to show aggression and so its owner offers it some food to try and pacify it. The dog likes to be stroked on the head and chest, but when it feels a hand move on to the back of its neck or shoulders it omits a menacing growl.

There are also a lot of things that the dog dislikes the owner doing: getting up to answer the 'phone; changing gear in the car; switching the gas fire on, are some examples.

After maturity the dog now sleeps where it wants and eats when it wants (often before its owner). It decides when it is time to play and when it is not. It has several possessions, which under certain circumstances it will allow other members of the household to borrow. It also decides what constitutes acceptable behaviour in its 'pack' and what is not acceptable; then, under the slightest provocation, eg., being brushed or made to lie down the dog will growl, snap or bite. Usually, by the age of two and a half, the dog is either **a)**. complete master in the house, making life difficult for the rest of the family, **b)**. has been cast out or put to sleep, or **c)**. is sent to a professional trainer for 'correction' or 'training'.

In this chapter we shall look further into upbringing with a view to attempting to encourage certain types of behaviour whilst suppressing undesirable traits.

Some Popular Myths

Whilst we are on the subject of canine behaviour patterns, it might help future understanding if I try and dispel some of the myths surrounding our canine friends.

It is often said that 'a dog will not bite the hand that feeds it'.
As we have already seen, some types of dogs under certain sets of circumstances are, in fact, more than likely to bite the hand that feeds than any other.

How about the phrase 'My dog understands every word that I say'
Again, as we will see in subsequent sections, nothing could be further from the truth. For a dog to become an obedience champion it needs to understand and obey only eight different commands: *heel, come, sit, stand, down, away, fetch and find* are probably the most commonly used. And yet, even with this comparatively small vocabulary, about ninety-five per cent of all dogs worked in obedience competitions never actually become proficient enough to attain the top level, Championship Test 'C'.

A dog has poor colour vision, seeing only in black and white and shades of grey and have a very poor visual memory. After an enforced absence from their owners, very few dogs would show any recognition if introduced on the other side of a vapour-proof glass screen. As soon as the dog is allowed to exercise its sense of smell, however, there is an immediate acknowledgement.

I have never seen anything that would lead me to believe that any dog has telepathic powers, nor have I met any person that can communicate to dogs through the power of telepathy although I myself, and many other trainers that I know could easily fool the average dog owner into believing that it were possible.

I have often witnessed events that have led owners to believe that their pets have such ability, but there has always been perfectly rational explanations of such events when one has some knowledge of a dog's very acute sense of smell and hearing.

I have never seen any dog suffering from schizophrenia, although many people, including several vets, will use this human condition to describe behaviour problems in dogs.

Dogs are not capable of human-type thought patterns, although most dogs will learn how to do things by trial and error and, sometimes through 'observational learning' coupled with a measure of good luck.

One of the fascinating things about dogs is the question of intelligence in connection with upbringing and training. We shall explore this in greater depth later, but for now it should suffice to say that an extremely intelligent dog is very difficult both to raise and train.

Breeds

The one big difficulty in writing a book on upbringing and training is that there are so many breeds, each with their own characteristics, and so many variations within each breed that even the best books are merely compromises. Not all training methods will work on any breed of dog. Some breeds require an expert understanding of how to adapt and apply the various techniques that have been developed and used in training other breeds.

Instructors at dog-training clubs, although carrying out an excellent service, usually only have personal experiences of training one or two breeds and even then they will pick only dogs with a particular temperament within their breed. I am sure that if a survey was carried out amongst all of the training instructors in the country, it would be found that nearly all of them own Border Collies, working sheep dogs or German Shepherds.

This is fine, of course, if you happen to have a dog of the same breed, but if you own a Kerry Blue Terrier, you may not find some of the instructors' methods very successful.

Mental Disorders

In my capacity as a professional trainer I am frequently requested to give advise on, or to train, dogs, displaying 'mental' disorders. With symptoms suggesting epilepsy or the more common teething fits, my advise is always seek veterinary help. As a general guide if the dog has just suddenly and inexplicably started to behave in an unpredictable and out of character fashion then a veterinary check up is called for. If, however, the dogs behaviour is slowly evolving into problems and it is merely displaying a worsening of existing behaviours then is is unlikely that the dog is suffering from a sudden or acute medical condition. It is very easy to label a dog mentally ill or unstable by using human terminology to describe the dog's actions when, in fact, the main problem can usually be identified as lying in one of three main areas:

1. *Upbringing.* The single biggest factor which influences the dog and its subsequent behaviour, particularly during the fourth to sixteenth week of life.

2. *Environmental Influences.* These are outside influences that might encourage natural instincts to develop in a manner that causes problems for owners. Joggers, for instance, attract all of the 'chase motivated' dogs. Once this instinct is aroused in an otherwise 'normal' dog, it may trigger off other problems such as chasing cars, motor cycles, etc.

3. *Temperament.* The dog's ability to cope with stress is both inherited and learnt from experiences and whilst an owner of similar temperament to his dog usually has little in the way of problems, an owner who is completely different in temperament might start labelling his dog as a behaviour problem, or mentally unstable.

All of these factors will be discussed in greater detail in this chapter. I would class a dog mentally ill or unstable for any behaviour that the dog displays at random without any logical reason, particularly displays of aggression.

Do You Own a Problem Dog?

What kind of dog do you own? An aloof Afghan Hound, a dominant Doberman, a boisterous Bearded Collie, or perhaps a mischievous mongrel?

Whatever the breed there may be certain behaviour traits, lying dormant, awaiting the correct time to surface in the dog's development from puppy hood to maturity.

During the past twenty-five years as a dog trainer, I have come across almost every conceivable type of behaviour problem ranging from the Cocker Spaniel that bit its owner every time the telephone rang, to the Doberman owner who rang in desperation asking me to stop his dog chasing helicopters!

As I've said it is extremely rare to find a dog that suffers from any form of mental disorder, even though some veterinary surgeons use human conditions to describe behaviour problems.

When we talk about behaviour problems we really mean behaviour that we, the owners, find undesirable or unacceptable in our dogs. For example, it is perfectly natural for any dog to use its teeth to defend itself when under threat. Unfortunately, we may find this behaviour unacceptable if Rover decides that the postman or the milkman poses a threat and uses his natural instinct to protect himself or his territory.

Most types of learned behaviour problems are easily reversible, provided they are dealt with in the early stages. Older dogs exhibiting serious problems can only be dealt with by professional trainers with a deep understanding of canine behaviour.

So how do you decide if you have a problem, or how serious your problems may get? Over the last twenty-five years I have developed a series of questions which I now ask all my clients on their first visit. This not only enables me to obtain an excellent view of what may be going on inside the dog's mind, but also tells me a lot about the owner and the relationship with the dog, which is vital if a cure is going to be effected. Read each question carefully and answer each one as honestly as you can.

1. Have you owned the dog from puppy hood?
2. What is the dog's age in months?
3. What time of day do you feed him?
4. Whilst eating his main meal, what would be his reaction if you plunged your hand into his bowl?
5. Where does he sleep at night?
6. What is the favourite toy your dog has to play with?
7. When he is not playing with his toys, where are they kept?
8. Will he allow you to groom him regularly?
9. Does he steal objects or items of clothing (not food)?
10. Are you happy with your dog's behaviour?

Let us have a look at the information to be gained from your response to the questions.

1. If you have had your dog since he was a puppy then any faults that he has are almost certainly due to you and the way that you have brought up your dog. If your dog was owned by someone else during the first five months of life, any problems you may have are more than likely due to its previous owner, who you may need to contact in order to ask them to fill in the questionnaire for you.
2. If your dog is under sixteen weeks old you will find it easy to remodel his behaviour. Between sixteen weeks and eighteen months (twelve months for toy breed) behaviour alteration is still possible, but takes time and a consistent effort on the part of the owner. Over eighteen months (twelve months for toy breeds) and you may well need professional help if you have problems with your dog.
3. Dogs should have set times for meals and should be allowed no more than ten minutes to eat their food, after which it should be taken up. If food is left down constantly the dog's appetite will be dulled and you will teach him to be very selective in what he eats. 'He will

only eat best steak' is an expression I often hear. What the owner really means is that my dog is spoilt and probably lacks respect for me as a person for allowing this situation to develop. A dog that is offered his food *before* the owners eat may well feel that he is the most important member of the pack, encouraging his dominance to develop.

4. A dog that will allow his owner to place their hand in his food without resentment shows trust and usually respect on the dog's part. You, the owner, can pat yourself on the back, for that trust must have been earned.

   Growling or snapping, i.e. being protective over its food may well be the first symptoms of dominance. In the first stages of dominance the dog will growl to see its owner's reaction. If the owner retreats then the dog has won the first round and, as he matures, will become more of a problem in this and other areas. Food aggression can also be a problem in its own right, with the dog showing no other signs of unacceptable behaviour.

5. Now that you have written down your answers to question 5, answer this one. Is this where you intended your dog to sleep when you first got him? If it is, then you have taught your dog correctly. He accepts that he is living within your territory. If he now sleeps on the bed, settee, by the fire, etc., where *he* wants to then not only have you given in to your dog at various stages during his upbringing, but your dog may well imagine that *you* are living within *his* territory. Finally, can you move your dog from where he is sleeping without touching him in any way? If you can then you clearly have a good measure of control over sleeping areas. If you cannot then your dog has good control over sleeping areas!

6. The most common toys are rubber rings (possession toys), balls (chase toys) and squeaky toys (killing toys), all of which are designed to satisfy natural instincts in our dogs. A lot of terrier type breeds would prefer a squeaky toy rather than a ball or rubber ring, because terriers have a highly developed instinct to grip with their teeth whilst shaking their prey.

The enjoyment of running after a thrown ball is commonest amongst most of the herding breeds, but not usually highly developed amongst the hounds.

Rubber rings (or occasionally balls or squeaky toys) used for possession or tug-of-war are fine providing the owner and not the dog controls the game. In other words if, during a game of tug-of-war, you can easily get the dog to give you possession of the ring or toy this is fine. If, on the other hand, you have difficulty in getting him to give up what he sees as *his* possessions, then you are almost certainly heading for trouble as your dog has already started to assert his dominance over you.

7. The large majority of dogs will leave their toys wherever they happen to finish playing with them. The more dominant dogs will generally take them to wherever they sleep and may even 'guard' them against removal by their owners. The more sensible owner will control the use of toys and will remove them, out of the dog's way at the end of a play session to assert *his* control and influence over the dog.

8. All dogs should be conditioned into allowing their owners to groom and when necessary to bathe them. If your dog will not allow you to brush him (the ears, back of the neck and the feet are 'sensitive' areas) then it shows that, from the early stages of puppy hood, you have shown your dog that you are not persistently strong-willed enough to be respected as 'pack-leader'.

9. This question is really a follow-on from question 6, as stealing slippers, socks, etc is just an extension of what the dog has learned to do with toys. There are three main causes of stealing from under the owner's nose:

a) For attention
b) To invite the owners to play a game of chase
c) For possession and removal to a 'safe' area

You should by now know which reason, if any, is behind your dog's thieving habits.

10. If you are not happy with you dog's behaviour, then it is up to you to change things. Dogs rarely improve their behaviour with age and may often get worse. Except in

certain cases, dogs are a product of their environment and upbringing and even the costliest puppies can, and do, turn out to have the most appalling anti-social behaviour given a poor upbringing.

Let us see how your dog measured up to the questions on his behaviour. Remember the accuracy of the analysis depends on your answers being truthful.

	Score		*Score*		*Score*
1. Yes	3	No	1		
2. Six weeks to six months	3	Six to eighteen months	2	Over eighteen months	1
3. Regular set time	3	Irregularly	1		
4. Accepts your hand	3	Growls	2	Snaps	0
5. Where you want	3	Where he wants	0		
6. Ring	3	Ball	3	Squeaky toy	3
6a. I can easily get the toy from my dog when I want	3			I cannot get the toy from the dog	0
7. Lying around the house	2	In his sleeping area	1	In my possession	3
8. Yes	3	No, he growls	2	No, he snaps	0
9. No	3	Yes, for attention	2	Yes, for possession	0
		Yes for play	2		
10. Yes	3	No	0		

Score

30–33   You may congratulate yourself on owning a well-adjusted, sensible, sociable dog.

23–29   Only one or two minor problems, which can be easily rectified, are preventing your dog from being the first-class champion that you desire.

18–22   The problems that you have need some careful

It is unfair to teach a puppy to jump up knowing that this behaviour will cause problems as the puppy grows

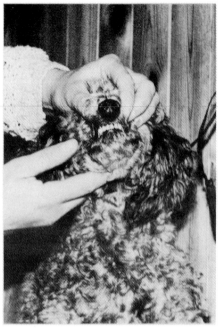

Rules should be established at the puppy stage

Examining your dog's teeth should be routine

Getting a dog accustomed to being groomed and handled is an extremely important lesson. If you cannot handle your own dog what chance does your vet have to treat him if he becomes ill?

All dogs should totally accept being touched whilst they are eating

It is almost impossible for a dog to distinguish between being allowed to chew slippers and toys but not being allowed to chew furniture etc

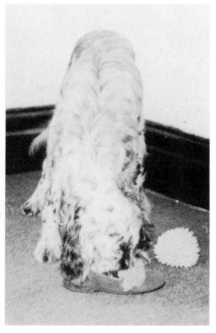

Who is taking who for a walk? The Gordon Setter is typical of so many dogs that have learned that the quickest way of getting from A to B is by putting their heads down and pulling

Some dogs learn to place one foot over the lead when they do not want to walk where the owner intends or to gain attention. The cure? Take no notice and keep walking

handling to prevent any future, more serious problems developing.

14–17   You quite definitely need help in rectifying your dog's behaviour as you may well find that he turns into a liability than a pleasure to own.

10–13   Your dog is already a headache and a liability to own; you may well need specialist help in order to change your dog's behaviour which will certainly get worse ultimately to the point where you may have to consider destruction.

Less than 10 You need professional help *fast* as you and your immediate family and friends are almost certainly in danger from your dog.

Now that we are exploring the relationship between dog and owner you might like to try the following test. This test will help you to determine just how easy your dog may be to train. Allow yourself just five minutes to complete the test and then work out your dog's behaviour score from the instructions that follow.

CANINE BEHAVIOURAL PROFILE

DOGS NAME: _____

Indicate your perception of your dog as a family pet by ticking one of the circles between each pair of words that best describes your dog. Only tick one circle for each pair of words and do so quickly without stopping to analyse your answers, the first response that comes to mind is undoubtedly the best.

For example if you tick the circle in column A for the first pair of words, this would indicate that you thought your dog was **VERY** touch *insensitive*, column B would indicate **FAIRLY** touch *insensitive*, column C would indicate **FAIRLY** touch *sensitive* and column D would indicate **VERY** touch *sensitive*.

	A	B	C	D	
touch insensitive	O	O	O	O	touch sensitive
bold	O	O	O	O	hesitant
demanding	O	O	O	O	giving
voice insensitive	O	O	O	O	voice sensitive
independent	O	O	O	O	dependant
leads	O	O	O	O	follows
spontaneous	O	O	O	O	disciplined
excitable	O	O	O	O	calm
dominant	O	O	O	O	submissive
controlling	O	O	O	O	controllable
frustrating	O	O	O	O	satisfying
overwhelming	O	O	O	O	laid back
relaxed	O	O	O	O	tense
confronting	O	O	O	O	avoiding
playful	O	O	O	O	boring
driving	O	O	O	O	coasting
wilful	O	O	O	O	compliant
competitive	O	O	O	O	uncompetitive
assertive	O	O	O	O	passive
frustrating	O	O	O	O	satisfying
quiet	O	O	O	O	noisy
annoying	O	O	O	O	likeable
mild	O	O	O	O	intense
people friendly	O	O	O	O	not people friendly
outgoing	O	O	O	O	clingy
bold	O	O	O	O	nervous
cheerful	O	O	O	O	sad
threatening	O	O	O	O	comforting
self assured	O	O	O	O	anxious
steadfast	O	O	O	O	shaky

SCORING

Add up all of the ticks in column A, all of the ticks in column
B, all of the ticks in column C and all of the ticks in column
D, write the totals underneath each column. Now add
together the totals for columns A and B and write down this

number. Then add together the totals for columns C and D and write this number down underneath the number you wrote for A and B. If you now subtract your C and D answer from the A an B answer the resultant number will give you a behaviour profile score, of between minus thirty and plus thirty.

WHAT IT MEANS

A score of between 0 and 10 would indicate a fairly well balanced dog and handler relationship which should be just about right for training purposes. The dog has a fair amount of character and is confident enough to adapt quickly to the training environment but controllable enough to make training relatively easy. This score would also indicate that the dog is quick to learn but also quick to pick up the wrong sort of associations if the handler does not remain one step ahead all of the time. The dog should certainly be a good prospect for the demands of competitive type training if that is what is required.

A score of between 11 and 20 would indicate a dog that was very quick to learn anything that was to its own advantage but one that was perhaps a little too self interested and independent to make training the dog an easy task. The handler would need to make changes in the relationship that they have with their dog so that they have greater authority over it. It is also possible that the handler will have to learn how to ration all rewards and privileges used so that the dog does not start to demand them as of right. A calm patient approach is required as well as lots of repetitive control based exercises early in the training programme.

A score of between 21 and 30 would indicate that the relationship between dog and owner is based on the dog being very firmly in control of all interactions that take place between them. Confrontational training techniques may well result in a worsening of the relationship with the possibility of aggression if the dog does not want to carry out requests such as lying down when told. It may be appropriate to seek behavioural advice so that measures that may be necessary to give the owner more control can be implemented at once.

This dog will be extremely fast at learning all of the things that you do not want it to learn and it is vital that the owner remains one step ahead of the dog at all times.

A score of between minus 1 and minus 10 would indicate a somewhat submissive dog that requires a gentle, more understanding approach to training. Although taking slightly longer to train, this dog should be capable of achieving a more consistent performance than most of the other, more confident types. This type of dog is usually more forgiving if mistakes are made in the early part of the training programme.

A score of between minus 11 and minus 20 would indicate a more nervous type of dog that is not at ease in anything other than the home environment. Although the dog will tend to excel at exercises where it is in close proximity to the handler, it may be on edge and mildly stressed in exercises that require working away from, or independently from the handler.

A score of between minus 21 and minus 30 would indicate a dog that is probably obsessively bonded to one person and although calm and easily controlled in its own safe home environment when there are no distractions, its behaviour changes rapidly when it is in a strange environment and there are distractions of people or even other dogs. Allow the dog some security by allowing a regular space that it may be allowed to retreat to if under stress. Introduce lots of confidence boosting exercises that allow freedom to explore the environment without stress. Individual behaviour counselling may be appropriate in some cases.

Behavioural Problems

Before we can attempt to alter anything that we find undesirable in our dog's behaviour, we have got to understand what it is that has caused the problem in the first place.

All puppies are born with much the same instincts, all of which are geared towards survival and reproduction. In some breeds, certain basic instincts have, by selective breeding, been exaggerated. Border Collies, for example are well known for chasing/herding instincts which can be further encouraged by careful training. Bloodhounds on the other hand, are best known for their ability to track a quarry using their nose.

The first thing to do is to find out as much as possible about the origin of the breed that you own and the purpose for which they were originally bred. It is then a good idea to allow your dog to exercise its natural abilities by training it to perform some tasks, rather than to allow him to devise something for himself as an outlet for his energy. A Border Collie trained to chase and retrieve a thrown ball is better than a Border Collie which has trained itself to chase a car!

Some of the easier problems to correct are jumping up, barking for attention, chewing and lapses in house cleanliness, but the principles involved may also apply to the more difficult areas.

Jumping Up

As with all learned behaviour, the responsibility for a dog jumping up rest firmly on the owner's shoulders! The way that this behaviour is usually started can be traced back to puppy hood. At a very early age the small puppy is actively encouraged to jump up and greet his owners at any time that the owners find convenient; coming into the house after a few hours' absence, kneeling on the floor and playing with the pup, allowing the pup to stand with its front paws on the settee when the owner is seated, etc. This then only starts to become a problem when a) the puppy grows in size; b) he starts to jump up at people other than his owner; c) when the dog is wet or muddy.

If owners made it a rule that only their best, light coloured clothes were to be worn in the vicinity of the puppy for the first six months of it's life with them then jumping up would never be a problem!

So how can we alter his behaviour? You may have tried pushing the dog back down every time that he jumps up. Despite your persistence this action will usually be ineffective because your hand contact is what the dog finds rewarding.

You can usually effect a complete cure by carrying out my instructions *consistently* each and every time your dog jumps up. You cannot teach a dog that it is acceptable to jump up under some circumstances and not others; it either is allowed to do so *all* of the time or *never.*

To start with simply turn your back on him and do not look at, speak to or touch your dog when he tries to jump up. Only give him some attention when all four feet are firmly on the ground. By consistently refusing to interact with him when he is jumping and only choosing to interact when he has his feet on the floor, you should begin to see a dramatic improvement within a few days.

For more persistent jumpers try the following: Allow your dog to jump up – you can even encourage him to do so. When his front paws touch you, take hold of one in each hand and *don't let him go down again.* Hold on for several minutes until he makes a really determined attempt to free himself, all of the time talking to him in an encouraging voice. He is not intelligent enough to know that you are the cause of his discomfort unless you make it evident, but it is not advisable; you want him to learn that it is his behaviour that is causing him to be in this predicament. When you release his paws, make him sit and then make a fuss of him.

Within a fairly short space of time the result will be that when your dog wants to greet you or anyone else, especially when it is excited, he will rush up and sit waiting for you to praise him. he will not risk jumping up because he will have learned that for some reason, when he jumps up he cannot get down again!

Some dogs try to remove the hands that are holding them by nibbling or biting. In this case, put something evil tasting on your fingers such as bitter aloes or hot chilli powder.

There is a second, much harsher alternative that you may use if the dog's physical size or weight make paw-holding impractical for you to carry out. Every time the dog jumps up, place one of your feet **gently** on one of his hind paws until the dog gets back down. As he does so make him sit and praise him well. Repeat each time and every time the dog jumps up, but please be careful not to cause any unnecessary discomfort.

Growling over food

There is never any excuse for a dog that growls over its food when someone approaches. The best way of preventing this from happening with a puppy or curing an older dog that growls is this. Place a collar and lead on the dog. Mix up his usual meal in his bowl, on a work surface whilst holding onto the lead. Place a few pieces of cooked liver, a few pieces of cooked chicken and a couple of pilchards near the bowl.

Place the food bowl on the floor and allow him to eat a few mouthfuls then turn and walk away from the bowl taking the dog with you. There is no need to say anything, it would be most unlikely for the dog to growl as you do not represent a threat. When the dog is well clear of the bowl, turn around, shorten the lead and walk back to the bowl, holding the dog slightly behind you. Pick up the bowl, place the liver on top and put it back down for the dog to eat. When the liver has been eaten, repeat the process using the chicken and then repeat once more using the pilchards. After a week it is usually possible to carry out the process off the lead with the dog only too happy to move back from his bowl when you approach, in anticipation of receiving some extra tasty treat. In milder cases, by feeding the dog out of three separate bowls spaced evenly on the floor, you will decrease the possibility of aggression occuring. Use the trick of picking one of the bowls up and placing something tasty on top of the food to get your dog to leave the bowl he was eating and to come to you for the bowl you are holding.

Barking for attention

Barking for attention is a similar type of problem which the owner will have instilled early in the dog's life. Like all associated problems it starts as a game, usually with one of the dog's toys. During a game, the dog becomes frustrated whenever its owner gains possession of the toy for more than a few seconds and it starts to whine or bark (some owners actually encourage the dog to bark by teasing it with the toy).

The dog is then allowed possession of the toy for a while before the process is repeated.

The same, attention seeking barking behaviour can also be learned in response to feeding and being stroked and made a fuss of.

As each day passes, the dog learns that it is the act of barking that produces the reward of either a toy, food or the subsequent attention of its owner. Shouts of 'be quiet' or 'shut up' make the game even more exciting, and so the problems get greater for the distressed owner who has to spend lots of time playing games or touching his dog to keep it quiet. Unfortunately, some dogs learn that any sort of attention can be had by barking constantly. Believe it or not, a short while ago someone contacted me who said that he had to stroke his dog constantly from the time he got in from work at 6.00pm until the time he went to bed at 10.30pm to prevent his dog from standing and barking at him.

The cure?

Every time the dog barks for attention, simply get up and walk out of the room and close the door behind you, leaving the dog devoid of anyone to play with. If this is repeated religiously each and every time that the dog barks and play or attention is only permitted after periods of complete silence, the dog should associate the act of barking with being left by himself for short periods, with silence being rewarded by play or attention, again replacing a bad habit with a good one.

A point worth making here is that however bad your dog's behaviour may be, *he* must find his actions rewarding, or he wouldn't repeat them. And so, in trying to alter behaviour, we must try and find what 'reward' the dog is getting for whatever problem we are trying to cure. It is then usually possible to remove the 'reward' aspect of the problem, thereby ultimately removing the problem itself.

The dog that barks when left alone in a room may find the act of its owner returning to shout or smack it preferable to being alone and may bark with renewed vigour in between brief visits by the owner to chastise it, as any attention is better than none.

The cure is to leave the dog in a room by itself for a short time whilst you are in the adjoining room. The moment you hear it bark either strike the door with the flat of your hand or open the door just far enough to put a water pistol through the gap and squirt it at the dog's nose. It is important that you do not shout at the dog when you do this as this would be considered giving the dog some attention.

The dog should soon associate barking at the door with the *door* becoming unpleasant. Every day there should be a time set aside to teach the dog to accept being left on his own whilst you are in the house. Unless the dog learns to accept this he will never be silent when you leave the house.

Chewing

The three main causes of chewing and their cures are:

1. *Boredom.* When left alone, even for short periods, the dog amuses itself by destroying various types of articles, the most common being wood, lino, carpet and leather. This usually starts at an early age and sometimes corrects itself with maturity. To stop the habit it is best to remove the cause. Remove all toys from the floor whenever the dog is left alone, treat all previously chewed surfaces with a preparation called Bitter Apple or any other taste deterrent (obtainable from your vet). Leave a large marrowbone for the dog to chew whilst he is alone. Worried about him taking the bone onto the furniture? Tie a piece of string around the bone and fasten the other end around any immovable object.

2. *Attention seeking.* The dog will steal something and run away to chew it up. This quite often occurs when the owner is engaged in some form of activity which does not involve the dog ie. answering the door, talking to someone, etc. Chasing the dog scolding him will generally not help: that is what he is doing it for – attention. Every time this happens, instead of chasing the dog get up and walk out of the room, leaving the dog behind. He will soon learn that instead of his behaviour gaining attention, it *loses* attention (the same rules apply for a dog which barks for attention).

3. *Insecurity*. With this problem the dog will selectively destroy things. Whenever it is alone it will want to have the presence of its pack leader (owner) very close at hand. In order to comfort itself the dog will usually select items most recently touched (or worn) by the owner, and will shred and lie on them. This form of chewing also indicates whom the dog regards as number one in its household. To correct this, try leaving an old jumper on or near the dog's bed every time it is left alone. This must be well handled and then every day left for the dog to lie on. (A glove is not big enough so the dog must shred it to form a bed.)

If all else fails, and provided that your dog is not chewing because it is under stress when it is left, you can buy a wire mesh cage, specially designed for dogs of various breeds, into which you can put your dog out of harm's way whenever he is left alone.

House cleanliness

If the owner of a young puppy is very careful about taking the pup out to relieve itself after every meal and every time that it wakes up after even the shortest nap then the house-training phase of a dog's development is usually complete in a matter of a few weeks. In some exceptional cases the process is reduced to a few days.

House training is in fact started by the mother of a litter of puppies, using her tongue to stimulate them to relieve themselves on waking and after feeding. As the puppies grow they attempt to venture further away to relieve themselves so as not to foul the nest area. The bitch, however, will clean up after the puppies to ensure that the sleeping area is always clean.

Some dogs unfortunately never learn to be clean at the 'nest' stage due to being either orphaned at or near birth or by having a mother that is not very house clean herself. On occasions, it is the owner of the bitch that is to blame by providing a whelping box or area that is too small, preventing puppies from being able to relieve themselves away from the sleeping area.

Problems will usually start to arise if the owner does not

spend enough time with the puppy during the first weeks in its new home, allowing 'accidents' to occur and consequently bad habits form. If the dog is taken out for a walk and then promptly relieves itself on the carpet when he gets home it is because that is what you (or its previous owner) have *trained* it to do!

Let us have a look at some of the more common problems relating to house training with a view to improving them.

Territory marking. This is usually a problem associated with the male dog approaching maturity or after. The problem is increased by using the dog at stud. The dog will 'mark' various items of furniture, etc, whenever one or a number of the following situations arise:

a) On 'strange' territory (someone else's house).
b) When a dog or bitch come into the house.
c) When anyone who comes into the house smells 'doggy', ie, has a dog of their own.
d) Whenever it gets the scent of a bitch in season (this can easily be detected by any dog up to six miles away!).
e) Whenever the house smells unfamiliar, ie, a new carpet is fitted.
f) When the owner comes home after being in the company of other dogs.

One way of preventing this annoying habit is to have the dog castrated by a vet. This needs to be carried out after the dog has fully matured. Most owners, however, are unwilling to take such steps to cure the problem and so a temporary solution is to use a female hormone injection or tablets.

Another way of solving this problem is to prevent the dog exercising his sense of smell, as it is the sniffing that triggers off the act of leg cocking. Every time that one of the above situations arises, put a dab of strong smelling ladies' perfume underneath the dog's nostrils. Carried out *consistently* this will break the habit or, at worst, improve matters.

Not clean through the night. By the time your dog is about sixteen weeks of age he should be clean when left alone for the night (approximately eight hours). Dogs above this age that still have accidents overnight do so out of habit rather than necessity. There are more obvious things to try, like feeding the dog in the morning instead of in the evening and then taking him out last thing at night to relieve himself, but usually these have little effect. Neither does smacking or rubbing the dog's nose in it. The latter course of action frequently teaches the dog to eat its own faeces!

Let me explain what happens when the dog is left for the night. In the early hours of the morning the dog will get up and walk away from his bed/basket and start sniffing at the floor for the familiar spot on which he will relieve himself. Once finished he will then return to his bed and settle down for the duration of the night. The cure comes in two parts.

First of all we must make it impossible for him to leave his bed, as it is extremely rare for a dog to foul the area on which it has to lie. To do this use a lead which has a good swivel on the end that attaches to the dog's collar, and fasten the other end to any immovable object. Alternatively you could use an indoor kennel. Leave the doors open between the room that your dog is in and the room where you are sleeping. If you hear a sound which suggests that your dog wants to go out and relieve himself then get up and accompany him to the garden, waiting until he has performed before going back to bed. Secondly, remove all traces of urine, etc, from the area away from his bed by cleaning with a solution of enzyme washing powder in solution with water or a product called *odour eliminator* (obtainable from your vet). Disinfectant will not suffice because it does not remove the smell is simply masks it by putting a stronger smell on top. Some ammonia based cleaners actually *cause* problems rather than curing them.

When you get up in the morning, go straight to your dog and release him and either take him out for a walk or let him into the garden. After two weeks remove the dog from the lead overnight, by which time a cure should be effected.

Another problem associated with house training is when the dog relieves itself at will during the day and night, sometimes in full view of its owner. To correct this habit all traces of urine smell must be removed, and established outside in an area that is acceptable for use as a toilet. The next time that the dog has an accident on the floor, mop up the urine with an adsorbent material (newspaper) and pick up the faeces and deposit them side by side on your selected area.

Treat carpets, lino, etc, in the dog's favourite areas in the house with your clean up solution of enzyme based washing powder and water. Take your dog out at regular intervals and walk him on the lead, backwards and forwards past your prepared site, allowing him to sniff at will. Do not take him back in the house until he has performed. Praise him well when he does. You may need to restrict him in his bed overnight for a week or so at night so to complete the twenty-four-hour cure.

If all else fails you can talk to your vet about the possibility of getting some behavioural or diet advice in order to cure the problem.

So for minor changes in behaviour, the rules to observe are as follows:

1. Find out as much as possible about the breed of the dog you own.
2. Define the problem you have and try to understand its cause.
3. Try to discover what part of the problem is rewarding for the dog.
4. Devise a method of removing the reward aspect of the dog's action.
5. Substitute the reward for modified behaviour.

Using these rules we shall now take a look at a typical minor behaviour problem.

Mrs Smith owns a Fox Terrier that shreds up letters as the postman pushes them through the letter box. Despite scolding the dog every time this happens, the problem is slowly getting worse. Taking the diagnosis and cure stage by stage we come up with the following answers:

1. Fox Terriers were bred to kill foxes and badgers in their underground haunts and part of the characteristics of the breed is that they should be quick, keen and alert and on tiptoe at the expectation of the slightest provocation.
2. The cause of the problem is the sudden appearance of a moving 'prey' preceded by the sound of the postman

walking down the drive and opening the letter box.
3. The reward is the killing/shredding process, made more exciting by the owner's attempt to steal the 'kill'.
4. The easiest way of making the kill unrewarding is to post a letter every day containing a couple of spoonfuls of hot chilli powder.You would then simply allow the dog to discover for himself how unrewarding his actions are when applied to letters.

As the dog's behaviour improves, a squeaky toy could be offered as a suitable reward for each occasion when the dog shows no reaction to the familiar sound of the post arriving.

The more serious problems of the dominant aggression over its owner, nervous aggression towards strangers and aggression towards other dogs are best left alone by the inexperienced owners and referred to a professional trainer specialising in behaviour problems.

Aggression

Dogs with aggressive tendencies fall into one or more of three categories.

a) Aggressive towards other dogs
b) Aggressive towards people other than its owner
c) Aggressive towards its owner(s)

Occasionally a dog will display all three types of aggression, but usually will exhibit only one. For example, the dog may be perfectly happy in the company of other dogs and totally reliable with its owners but will not tolerate the presence of strangers.

Aggression towards other dogs

This category can be further divided into:

Fear-associated biting
Sexual aggression
Chase-motivated aggression
Dominant aggression (territorial)

Fear-associated biting. This is learnt at an early age and can sometimes be taught by the puppy's mother. More often it is the result of a direct act of aggression at the hands (or teeth) of another dog. For example, when the young pup is taken for a walk a dog rushes out from an open garden gate and attacks the puppy. Because the pup is restricted on the lead it cannot escape. As the pup grows both physically and mentally, signs of aggression towards other dogs (and bitches) become more and more evident. This often happens only when the dog is on lead and, much to the owner's surprise, the dog appears friendly with other dogs when off the lead. The reasons for this revolve around the owner. As he becomes aware of his dog's aggression every time he sees another dog approach when out for a walk, he tightens the lead in order to try and control his dog's expected aggression. The dog, now feeling he is unable to retreat from the advances of the approaching dog, has only one option – move the other dog out of the way before it comes too close. The handler, by tightening the lead, is unwittingly giving his dog the signal for aggression. To remove these aggressive tendencies it is absolutely vital that the dog is trained to walk to heel *correctly*, ie, on a completely slack lead (see 'Walking to heel' page 103). In addition to teaching your dog to walk correctly on the lead it is also important that your dog is given lots of opportunities to socialise with other, friendly dogs. Taking out all of the dogs daily food allowance and giving small portions as other dogs approach will help to reduce the level of aggression whilst teaching a pleasant outcome to future encounters.

If this is repeated each and every time that the dog first spots another dog the result should be that the tendency to move towards other dogs will diminish because of the anticipation of a reward coming from the handler. The dog should then be more relaxed in the knowledge that he is not being restricted by a tight lead which cuts off the possibility of an escape should any dog venture too close.

A taste deterrent or water pistol squirted on the dog's nose as he moves forward sometimes meets with a fair degree of success. The only problem encountered is that few people have the necessary technique or timing to apply the correction at the correct psychological moment.

Sexual aggression. This is almost exclusively confined to male dogs. Early symptoms include a desire to mount objects such as cushions, children and people's legs. Lots of owners then think that the dog 'needs a bitch to mate in order to calm him down'; this unfortunately will usually make matters worse. The dog will then start to approach other dogs either on or off the lead, stalking up on tiptoe in order to make himself look as tall as possible, and sniff them to determine the sex. If the dog is male and shows signs of submission it may escape an attack. Growling, a direct stare or running away will usually be sufficient to provoke an attack. If the animal is a bitch, then it may be subjected to attempts to mount even though it is not in season. The dog may also jump up at children, knocking them over in attempts to mount them and showing aggression if they resist.

Some dogs even attempt to mount their owners and show aggression if the owner tries to push them off. The scent of a bitch will increase aggression, and it therefore follows that incidents of dogs biting other dogs and people are at a peak around the end of April to the middle of June, as more dogs reach maturity at that time due to the fact that, traditionally, puppies are bred for Christmas sales. Few breeders aim to sell puppies in June or August as most people are reluctant to take on a puppy then because of holiday commitments.

If you suspect that your dog has sexually motivated aggression tendencies, the best course of action is to consult your vet with a view to hormone therapy or castration. Providing the operation is carried out when the dog is mature (and not before) all of the characteristics of the male are retained without the worry of sexually provoked attacks. I am greatly in favour of the operation as a cure for this type of problem and I do not know why some people are willing to put themselves, their children, other people and dogs at risk when the solution is so simple. There are an increasing number of vets who advocate castration at sixteen weeks of age because it is easier and there is less risk of post operative trauma. It is certainly worth thinking about if your puppy is merely a family pet and you have no wish to breed from him or for him to father some of the growing number of unwanted puppies. It is widely accepted in the horse world that geldings are easier to handle than stallions. Why then the reluctance to castrate a sexually aggressive dog?

Chase-motivated aggression. Some dogs have a highly developed chase instinct and learn that quite a lot of fun may be had by chasing after other dogs and giving them a nip as they run away. Typically, the dog will leave its handler at great speed when it sees another dog which may even be several hundred yards away. Despite the frantic shouts of its owner the dog maintains its course and runs directly at the other dog. If the other dog is taken by surprise at the sight of the another dog hurtling towards it and takes flight, the chasing dog will continue to run after and terrorise it.

If, however, the other dog acts aggressively by standing his ground and possibly growling, the chasing dog breaks off his 'attack' and heads back towards its owner, tail between legs. With this sort of problem the dog will usually be perfectly all right when passing other dogs on the lead. Unfortunately, the owner again makes matters worse by exercising his 'aggressive' dog only when he know he is unlikely to encounter other dogs. It follows that when the eagle-eyed owner spots another dog he recalls his own dog and puts it on the lead immediately. After several such repetitions a clever dog will learn that when its owner shouts 'Rover come' it means that there is a dog to chase somewhere and, instead of returning to its owner, it will search for and chase the intruder.

The simple solution is to teach a running recall and also, as an outlet for the dog's chase instincts, teach it to retrieve a ball.

The sequence of events should then be, when the dog is exercising free and another dog comes into view, recall him and throw the ball for him to retrieve. Once again a clever dog will soon learn that a ball is better than other dogs when it comes to chasing (see Toys, page 24). If the dog proves particularly stubborn you could try an avoidance learning technique such as getting a friend with a trained dog to meet you in the exercise field and let if off the lead. Introduce your dog at the opposite end of the field and let him off the lead. As he races towards your friend and his dog, give your recall command. Your friend then simply gives your dog a little surprise as he approaches such as, emptying a bucket of cold water on his head, firing a starting pistol, throwing a plastic lemonade bottle with a few pieces of gravel inside towards him, etc. If carried out correctly your dog should associate chasing other dogs with an event that is too disturbing to make it worth the effort involved. However, you will still need to teach your dog to chase and retrieve a ball as an outlet for this instinct, otherwise he might turn his aggression to joggers, cars, bicycles, etc.

Dominant aggression (territorial). If you have a really dominant dog or bitch you may well experience problems of aggression with other dogs regardless of whether or not your dog is on or off the lead. Any dog that it sees on its territory will be threatened and if necessary attacked. Your dog will adopt the dominant position ie, push his head and neck across the other dog's shoulders to assert his/her superiority. All of his senses are fixed on the other dog in order to interpret the posture and signals conveyed by it. If you have a male dog he will usually urinate on any available marking post if his access to the other dog is restricted by the lead. This he will do if the approaching dog's signals are submissive in nature. If the other dog resists your dog's dominant posture both dogs will freeze and the slightest movement by either will start a fight. If the fight is between two extremely dominant dogs, or worse still bitches, very serious damage can easily take place. If the owner tries to separate the two dogs he is quite likely to be badly bitten in the confusion that ensues.

This is not an easy problem to solve and is made worse if you own more than one dog as the more dominant will protect the other, more submissive pack member. By far the best way is to teach the dog to carry out a behaviour that is not compatible with aggression for example to lie down on command or to hold a favourite toy in its mouth. You will also need to make yourself a lot more dominant over your dog. Another helpful procedure is to insist on the absolute minimum of territory marking consistent with the dog being allowed to relieve itself. It is not necessary for a dog to mark *every* lamppost and street corner on a walk. If you reduce the amount of territory marking you may well reduce the territory that the dog defends.

Remember that if you adopt the correct methods of upbringing and are careful about the early social contact that your puppy has with other dogs little difficulty will be experienced. Some dogs when deprived of all social contact with other dogs at an early age will never learn the correct social signals and body language and will be a target for acts of aggression by other dogs and then become fear biters.

Aggression towards people other than its owners

We can subdivide this category into:

Nervous aggression
Territorial aggression
Chase-motivated aggression
Dominant aggression

Nervous aggression. This is the most common reason for dogs being labelled dangerous or vicious. There can be many causes for nervous aggression; it may well be a characteristic which has been learned from the puppy's mother. When the puppies are confined with her, they will learn various social signals from her.

Suppose the bitch is nervous about the approach of a stranger and warns anyone off by growling/barking/snapping. As the puppies grow and move to new homes they retain their learned mistrust of strangers and barking, growling, etc, becomes progressively worse as the pup grows older. Most owners, when they realise that the puppy dislikes strangers and in the early stages will run and hide, will attempt to force the pup to be more friendly by dragging it towards anyone it appears to be frightened of. Worse still are the attempts by strangers to get the pup to come to them by staring at it and holding out their hand. As far as the pup is concerned a direct stare constitutes a challenge, and therefore makes it even more wary of the approach. When a hand is extended the pup learns that by snapping in self-defence the hand and threat is withdrawn. Its behaviour has been successful and so it gets worse as it gets older. When taken out for a walk, if the owner stops to talk to anyone or sometimes even on the approach of a stranger, the dog will raise the hair on the back of its neck, move forward to the end of the lead then freeze and bark or growl furiously. Attempts to win the dog's confidence make matter progressively worse to the point where the dog starts biting. The dog's aggression is, to a large extent, dictated by the signals conveyed by the approaching person. It is a complete mistake to offer a dog the back of your hand to sniff. Do this to a nervous dog and you will get it bitten. Looking it in the eyes and calling its name and trying to coax it also put the dog on the defensive. Sadly, a lot of owners think that the dog is protecting them – it often isn't, it is protecting itself. If it were off the lead it would probably end up hiding behind the owner's legs, still barking.

The universal 'cure' of hitting the dog for barking cannot possibly work – it only serves to make the poor dog even more determined to keep people away from it at all costs. This sort of dog will, incidentally, form a very strong almost obsessive bond with a member of its own household. Unfortunately, the longer the problem is left the harder it is to cure. A fear biter can easily see someone coming into its immediate territory as a threat so serious as to be a matter of life and death, and it may well 'think' that its very existence is dependent on its ability to defend itself. Bites from a nervous aggressive dog are usually fairly serious. Let me explain why.

Let us look at the same problem from a human viewpoint. Assume that you are the person with a fairly nervous disposition. Someone bursts into your living room, stares at you, shouts, raises his fist in what you take to be a threatening manner. He then starts to approach you. What options are you faced with? Well, you could run and hide but suppose your escape route was cut off by a member of your family who physically prevented you from running? There are only two options left now, namely to submit and let him hit you (or so you believe) or to hit him before he has a chance to strike you. As you cannot escape him you must drive him away from you.

Imagine now that this sort of apparent threat took place

fairly regularly. As soon as you realise that your act of self-defence aggression caused the person to leave you alone or leave hurriedly you would, of course, repeat the behaviour whenever you felt it necessary. Would you not also be more likely to show aggression if threatened if you had a 'minder' standing behind you to back you up?

Human beings are, of course, able to communicate to one another using powers of speech, and therefore misunderstandings in terms of aggression are easier to resolve without resorting to violent means. It is a far more difficult task to communicate effectively with a nervous dog, often because the wrong sort of logic is applied to the canine mind. It is also a fact that when a dog is highly stressed by a situation then it is not in a position to learn very much about how to control it's fear but will merely react through the self preservation instinct.

So how can we alter a nervous aggressive dog's behaviour?

Let us deal with behaviour in the house first. Avoid any direct confrontations with anyone outside the immediate family when they enter the house. Put the dog into another room before allowing the person in. Instruct them not to try and talk to the dog or even look at it, just totally ignore it. Attach a six-foot lead to the dog's collar, but not to hold the lead or try to restrict him in any way. Let the dog into the room where the visitor is seated, leaving the door open.

It is likely that the dog will rush in barking and stop several yards short of the 'intruder'. When he realises that a) there is no threat from the person, b) he is not being restricted and c) that his 'minder' is not backing him up, he will probably reduce the amount of barking and settle as close to his owner as possible. Once the initial barking has subsided you should then pick up the end of the lead, walk over and place it in the other person's hand. Walk away from your dog and tell the person to slowly pull him towards them, still without eye or voice contact. The dog, realising that it is fastened to the 'intruder' will now focus all of its attention on *avoiding* any confrontation and will very quickly settle down. If you repeat this sequence each and every time anyone comes into the house the dog will soon learn to disregard any apparent threat and will accept anyone. If you then instruct the person to take a toy out of the toy box (see 'Toys') and encourage the dog to show interest or alternatively use some tasty tidbit to offer the dog, the result will be that a) the dog will learn that anyone entering the house at your request does not constitute a threat. The only problem with this treatment is that your dog could easily start to pester everyone that comes in either for food or a game with a toy!

I should also add that the dog should be taken out of the room before anyone gets up to leave, otherwise, particularly in the early stages the dog may well display aggression to 'chase away' the intruder.

The same method can be adopted outside, by handing anyone the lead if the dog is inclined to bark at them. To do this always have the person walking *in the same direction* as you are facing. You should avoid handing the lead to anyone standing directly in front of you as the dog could easily take this as being a challenge or threat and may take steps to defend itself.

Territorial aggression. A lot of dog owners are aware of the obvious benefit of owning a dog which exhibits a degree of territorial aggression. Generally speaking, the smaller the area of territory the stronger the dog's instinct to protect it. A dog that is very friendly with people in the local park can appear to be really ferocious if it is left in the owner's car. The approach of a stranger will trigger off the most menacing barking, growling and teeth baring imaginable.

Sometimes, a dog's territory may extend into areas that make him a distinct liability, encompassing not only the house and garden but also the road beyond the garden gate and even the local park or exercise field. He will then attempt to chase away anyone found encroaching in his area.

There are several ways to deal with the problem, but here is the tricky part. You must be absolutely certain that your dog's problem *is* territorial aggression, as it is easy to make your dog's problem of aggression much worse by using an inappropriate method of correction.

The first thing to do is to eliminate the area that the dog sees as his territory by having seven different exercise areas for each day of the week. Because of the small irregular amounts of time he spends in each, the dog will not associate any of the areas as being his. With a male dog, preventing him lifting his leg when on the lead will also help eliminate marking out areas of territory and subsequently defending them against 'intruders'.

Teaching the dog to carry out an instant 'Down' can also be used to alter the dog's basic behaviour, because obeying the command he will not be in a position to act in a aggressive manner. The handler then leaves the dog in the down position and insists that he remains there for the duration of any interaction. The dog should quickly learn to leave territory defence to the responsibility of its owners.

Chase-motivated aggression. This sort of behaviour is exhibited when the dog chases and nips at anyone moving away from him. I emphasise the word nip because the dog is never intent on damaging the quarry. The people most at risk are cyclists, joggers, etc., where the dog is encouraged by the fact that if he runs up to nip, people usually accelerate making the 'game' even more exciting.

One way of stopping his behaviour is to make the game of chasing people completely unrewarding by any one of the following methods:

1. Have the jogger armed with a bucket of cold water to tip onto the dog as he approaches.
2. Give the jogger a starting pistol to fire as the dog approaches.
3. Leave a twenty-foot line attached to the dog and have the jogger pick up the lead when the dog approaches and then prevent the dog from returning to its owner by dragging it away behind some obstacle, out of sight of its owner. After a minute or so the dog, now worried that it may never see him again, can be released to rejoin its owner. This method is particularly effective.

In any of the above methods it is important that a ball is thrown when the dog returns, which is an agreeable and acceptable alternative to chasing people. It is also a good idea occasionally to call the dog back when it is half way

between you and the ball thereby totally controlling the
dog's chasing instinct.

Dominant aggression. For a dog to exhibit signs of dominant
aggression towards people other than its owner it must also
exhibit signs of the same dominant aggression with its
owners; to all intents and purpose curing the problems of
dominance with owners should also stop this form of aggression with other people – while its owners are there. With
this form of aggression the best policy to adopt is to ensure
that the owners remain in attendance where strangers come
into contact with the dog.

Typically, when the owners leave the dog alone with someone it will strut up to them and start to intimidate by pushing
them with its shoulders and generally bullying them around
physically. It may also go right up and stare at them, inviting
conflict, or growl in a very menacing manner.

It is rare for the dominant dog to bite people other than
its owners – it never needs to!

Aggression towards its owners

This is by far the most common form of aggression and
probably the biggest single reason for dogs being destroyed.
It is also one of the most misinterpreted forms of aggression
by dog trainers and behaviourists alike.

People use a variety of terms to explain this behaviour:
schizophrenia, rage syndrome, highly strung, interbred, etc.
None of these terms, however, explain why dogs become
aggressive only towards their owners! As far as I am concerned, if I can shed any light on the subject then this book
is immediately justified.

Let us start by looking at some common factors involved
in the problem, regardless of breed or sex.

1. All dogs that are aggressive towards their owners must
   have played tug-of-war as puppies and learned that in
   games of strength they were superior.
2. Growling during such games induced the owner to growl
   back and 'fight' harder.
3. All dogs with this problem have usually stolen possessions

they should not have had and run away to a safe place to encourage conflict and to 'teach' the owner their position within the 'pack'.

4. It is *not* an accident that when Dad gets up to make a cup of tea, the dog will deliberately go and sit in *his* chair even though there are other vacant chairs in the room (no, it is not because the seat is warm)! Then when Dad comes back in and tries to get the dog to move it growls at him or bites him if he puts his hand on it to get it to move.

5. Most dogs with this problem have 'conditioned' their owners to not only feed them *before* the family sit down for their main meal but they often also conditioned the owners to offer more and more tasty food, often refusing what is placed down for them and holding out for something better . . .

6. The dog must want to obtain control of either the bedroom and/or the bed or any other comfortable areas in the house. It is interesting to note that sometimes the owners have conditioned their puppies to accept that growling over food is not tolerated and so being possessive over food may *not* be a problem, but often is.

So how can you alter this behaviour? This is where most trainers incorrectly advocate the use of force, but just look at what the dog's behaviour is leading towards – conflict. Your dog will be only too pleased to demonstrate his superior strength when challenged, and it is rare for any dominant dog to back down. How about the trainers who advocate picking the dog up, staring at it and shaking it till it gives in? Ask the trainer to demonstrate this method with a dominant aggressive dog *in its own home* and he will end up in hospital! Of course, a lot of people tell me that although the dog may growl, "He knows who the boss is" How right they are!

The answer to the dominant dog is in altering the owner's behaviour towards his dog in stages and thereby obtaining a corresponding behaviour change in the dog. Although the programme must be tailored to the individual dog, the following stages should nearly always be effective in drastically improving this behaviour.

Week 1 Take *all* of the dog's toys away from him and keep them where he has no access to them for the duration of this programme. Move all items that he is likely to steal out of his way. Ignore him as much as possible if *he* wants attention. Allow the dog to play games with the toys that are now denied him (your toys now, not his). Each game ends with you putting your toys away.

Week 2 Move the dog's sleeping quarters as far away from the bedroom and living room as possible. For the rest of the dog's life he is never allowed access to any bedroom again – even whilst they are being vacuumed!

For the rest of his life maintain the following feed pattern. Mix up the dog's food just before the family sit down for their main meal of the day but put it up on the work surface out of his reach. Eat your own meal, ignoring him. When the table has been cleared, offer him his food. Remove anything that remains in his bowl after ten minutes.

Week 3 Attach a twelve-foot-long piece of thin cord to the dog's collar and let the dog trail it around the house wherever he goes all of the time there is anyone at home. Now leave as many things that the dog is likely to steal around the place and let him steal them and run away. Now without shouting at him, or reprimanding him in any way, pick up the end of the line and pull him gently towards you. When he is close to you, tell him he is a good boy and take the object off him quietly. If he objects then try the same technique but this time using one of his favourite toys. Continue until you have complete control before using one of the more highly prized items that he likes to steal. He will obviously learn, in a very short space of time, that he can *never* win any more possession games.

Week 4 Keep the line attached and now, whenever he gets on your chair, etc, and you want to move him, simply pick up the end of the line and pull him towards you calling him by name. Reward him with the words good boy etc. when he does as you request. It also helps if, whilst he is relaxed by the fire or in his basket, you gently pull him towards you then go and sit in his sleeping area.

Week 5 Dispense with the twelve foot line and replace it with an ordinary three foot lead. As part of his daily routine, lift him onto a small table, fasten the lead to any sort of fixture and the dog's collar. Brush him all over, paying particular attention to behind his front and back legs. Completely ignore any objectionable behaviour, and don't say one word to the dog – he cannot escape and the more he struggles the quicker he will tire himself out. As soon as you have finished brushing him, feed him. He will soon learn to accept and even enjoy these sessions because they are followed by something pleasant. Being groomed on the owners terms now no longer constitutes a challenge and he cannot avoid the procedure by showing aggression.

Week 6 Dispense with the lead, only replacing it should the dog start to regress.

So there you have it. If you really think about it carefully you will see that in order to reverse the order of dominance all we have done is to play the games of dominance in reverse. We are teaching the dog behaviour that he has been trying to teach us using the same games!

To everyone's advantage, the one thing that almost every puppy learns is that when the lead is attached the owner, or the person holding the lead, is stronger. Remember the first few times you took the pup for a walk on a collar and lead and he fought against it? Well, he quickly learned that when he was on the lead he *had* to go where you wanted. Logical isn't it?

3

Training and Learning

How does a dog learn?

How does a dog, or for that matter, any animal, learn how to carry out an action in response to a command given by the trainer? What are the factors that govern how quickly or accurately the dog learns to respond to such a command? Why do some people make better trainers than others? And why are some dogs apparently difficult to impossible to train?

In order to understand the answers to these and other related questions, I shall attempt to explain, from personal experience, the way that I see the working of a dog's mind. The following pages are written from a serious study undertaken at first hand, and are not merely copies or extracts taken from reference books on animal behaviour and psychology. I did once read a paper given to students undertaking a university degree course. The paper was entitled "How to Train Animals" and gave instructions on the theory involved in getting an animal (dog, rat, pigeon, etc.) to carry out a fairly simple task at a given signal from the trainer.

The theory involved was extremely complex and the training was broken down in stages so that by the time one had reached the concluding paragraph it was assumed that the reader, if he followed the text, would end up with the desired result.

The only problem, sound as the theory may have been, was that the author had obviously never actually trained an animal in his life – nor could he have done if his paper was anything to go by. His error was that his methods did not take into account the individuality of the subject under training and he assumed that all of the correct associations would be made at each and every stage of the process. The question "what if this happens?" never arose. It was assumed that problems would not be encountered.

Whilst my ideas on behaviour may not agree with accepted theory, I can claim to have an extensive *practical* knowledge of canine behaviour, having dealt with hundreds of so-called 'problem' dogs of all ages and breeds. I am also one of the very few behaviourists who is also involved on a day to day basis with training dogs, and competing with the dogs that I own. The theory behind training dogs is therefore continually updated and is not how I think I remember how I had trained dogs many years previously!

A Russian scientist called Ivan Pavlov pioneered the research into our understanding of how animals learn. He found that by offering a dog some food (*natural stimulus*), an increase in the flow of gastric juices in the digestive tract was apparent (*natural response*). Further to this, he experimented by sounding a bell immediately prior to offering the dog food and observed that, after a number of repetitions, the sound of the bell alone (*conditioned stimulus*) was enough to increase the production and flow of gastric juices (*conditioned response*).

Association is the basis of learning in order for a dog (or any animal) to learn to carry out any action, the stimulus and response must be contiguous (happen closely together in time). We associate thunder and lightening as one because they tend to happen closely together, ie. the flash of lightening followed by the roll of thunder. If the lightening was followed ten days later by the clap of thunder, we may not guess that the two events are linked.

So for an association between two events to be linked, we must ensure that they are contiguous. In order to strengthen an association, we can use *reinforcement*. This can be either positive (usually a reward **given** to the dog), or negative (the **removal** of an unpleasant stimulus).

Using the sit command as an example, let us see how this all fits in together. We give the command: 'Fido *sit*' (stimulus) and immediately push his romp onto the floor (response), and as soon as he is in the desired position we offer him a tidbit (positive reinforcement). If the dog makes all of the correct associations, in a short space of time the command *'sit'* will make the dog respond by taking up the sit position in anticipation of the food reward.

The second method involves again giving the command 'Fido *sit*' (stimulus), but this time he is struck lightly on the rump until he adopts the desired position (response). When he is sitting the force that was applied to his rump is removed (negative reinforcement). In a very short space of time the dog learns that on the command *'sit'* he is to adopt the sit position to avoid a smack on the bottom.

Armed with a basic knowledge of how our dog is able to learn to 'understand' commands, let us take a closer look at each of the components of learning.

Conditioned stimulus

This is most commonly a particular word whose meaning is often descriptive of the action required by the dog eg. 'sit', 'down', 'come', etc. The word of command itself is unimportant as dogs have no recognition of meanings of individual words or sentences. Even the higher primates such as chimpanzees and gorillas are unable to string together groups of 'words' to transmit information.

Short words of command should be used whenever possible and they should all have an individual sound, in order to minimize the risk of the dog misinterpreting like-sounding commands. A dog training to associate command 'no' with displeasure may easily get confused if trained to carry out a competition sendaway using the command 'go'. In this instance, a command 'away' would be a better alternative as there is less risk of misunderstanding on the dog's part. The control of tone and pitch are essential when delivering commands, which is why one should not attempt any training when in a bad mood because of the voice and facial expression changes. A person with a monotone voice would not generally be very successful in training a dog to spoken commands. Compulsion commands trained by negative reinforcement ('down', 'no', etc) are normally given in a low-pitched tone, as the majority of dogs are reasonably submissive towards lower frequency noise. (A dog is more likely to be disturbed by the beat of a bass drum than a high frequency whistle.)

As an alternative to spoken commands, signals may be used. These are most commonly given by hand and can be just as successful as spoken commands, but have the disadvantage of having to be seen by the dog before they can be obeyed. It is not practical to train a dog to do a recall to handler on a visual signal, because if he is heading off in the opposite direction the dog will never know that he is being recalled, unless of course, he looks round.

Although unnecessary, lots of trainers use a combination of command and signal to transmit commands to their dogs. In training a dog to go into the down position the handler might use the command 'Fido down' and simultaneously point to the ground.

The only problem with this is knowing which stimulus the dog is accepting – the command, the signal or the combination of command and signal.

The use of whistles of varying pitch is highly successful as a means of stimulating a dog to carry out a particular action. Anyone who has watched a shepherd working his dog to a whistle will understand its effectiveness, particularly at a distance.

A whistled command has an advantage over spoken commands as, once a dog has been trained to carry out some action to a note from a whistle, it does not matter who blows that whistle as the dog should obey regardless, whereas a dog trained to a spoken command needs to hear not only the sound, but also the correct tone.

If you are going to use a whistle to train your dog then it is important that you use one specifically manufactured for the purpose. Gundog training whistles are about the best and you will find a number stamped on the back of the whistle which refers to the pitch. Make sure that, if you lose the whistle once your dog is trained, you get a whistle with the same number on the back otherwise your dog may well misinterpret the sound.

There are other ways of transmitting information to a dog, touch and smell being just two. Few people would even dream about exploiting these areas, even though they would readily accept that a dog's principal sense is its sense of smell.

Conditioned response

This varies from a simple single act on the dog's part to a response such as 'sit', meaning put your bottom on the floor, to a more complex response which requires several different actions, carried out in the correct order to a single command such as 'find', meaning go and use your nose to locate an article bearing a particular scent, then pick it up and return without dropping it and sit 'presenting' to the handler until told to release.

The response to a command might take anything from a second to execute, eg, 'down', up to and sometimes exceeding thirty minutes. eg, tracking.

A lot of so-called problem dogs have taught themselves or have been inadvertently taught by their owners to respond to a particular action or sound, for example, the Bearded Collie that bites its owner every time he changes gear whilst driving his car. A conditioned response can be extinguished, more or less successfully depending on the degree of conditioning. Most people who work with their dogs in competition will agree that by allowing an inexperienced handler to work their dog, in a short space of time the dog loses its response to commands; it is effectively untrained.

Association

This is really the key to learning and the success of any dog-training programme depends on the dog making all of the correct associations between command and action required in order to learn to carry out instructions from its handler. As we have already seen, the timing between command and action required is crucial if the dog is to make the correct associations in order to learn and carry out a command.

Squeaky toys may serve to reinforce a dog's instinct to kill. The dog will shake and bite the toy, often growling at it and becoming very excited. Play with such toys is therefore best kept under the owner's control

Two very typical examples of dominant aggression towards owners started by games of possession with a rubber ring

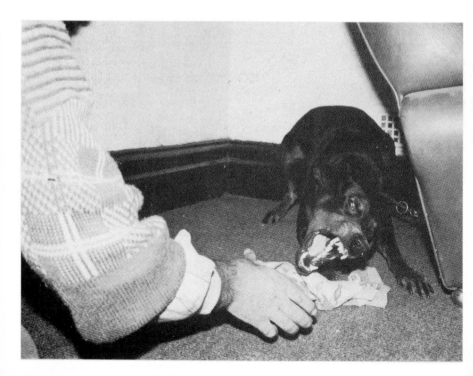

The same game of possession but played to a different set of rules. The pup can never win the game with the child's rubber ring and will never therefore try to dominate him

Nervous aggression. The Jack Russell on the left looks terribly aggressive whilst the lead keeps him away from the Dobermann who is quite submissive. Off the lead he would keep his distance without display of aggression at all; he may even play with the other dog

Compare the aggressive dog (*left*) baring its teeth to warn of intent to bite with the submissive dog (*right*) 'grinning' at its owner

Using the sit command we will now examine all of the possible associations that the dog may have during the learning phase. We shall start or experiment by walking our dog in the local park, on the lead, on our left-hand side. At intervals we will stop and give Fido a command to 'sit' and at the same time we will push his bottom to the floor and reward him with a food treat. After many repetitions Fido starts to respond to the command 'sit' and no longer requires a hand on his rump to get him into the 'sit' position.

A week of training goes by and sure enough Fido will now sit every time he hears the command, and so we can pat ourselves on the back in the knowledge that Fido now understands the command 'sit'. Or does he? If we now let Fido off the lead to run and exercise and when he is twenty yeards away we command 'Fido sit' we find to our surprise that we get no response at all.

At home when Fido is lying down near the fire we command 'Fido sit' and find that he makes no attempt to get up into the sit position. On a visit to the local vet we might walk into the waiting room, sit on a chair to wait our turn and command 'Fido sit' and again he responds as though he does not understand what is required.

A lot of people would say that Fido knows what is required but is defiant; this is not the case. Fido really does not associate the *command* 'sit' with the action of putting his bottom to the floor.

The association that Fido has with the command is that whilst walking in the park at a particular spot on the handler's left-hand side, on the lead, when the handler stops and gives a command of 'Fido sit' he is to put his bottom on the floor. In the absence of any of the above associations Fido might well fail to understand the command. For example, walking Fido in a different park or walking on the handler's right-hand side or off the lead or giving the command 'sit' whilst continuing to walk forward, we would probably find that Fido would not respond because the associations that he has with the command are limited to where the initial training associations took place.

So, in order to train Fido to understand the command

of 'sit' we must ensure that our training programme is structured to give him the experience to react to the command alone without regard to the environment and circumstances surrounding it. In other words, the command 'sit' must be the primary association with the action required and we must work to eliminate, as far as possible, all of the secondary associations.

Very few trainers are capable of training a dog to carry out a command under any circumstances. Almost every week at obedience competitions you can witness some of the country's top dragging their owners from the car park to the obedience ring where they perform the most beautiful heelwork, and then leave the ring at the end of the test only to drag their poor owners all the way back to the car park. They have been trained to understand the command only near or within the confines of an obedience ring, at a training area or in the local dog club hall.

Some trainers may indeed think that they have trained their dog to obey various commands but have in fact, conditioned their dogs to a number of secondary associations. Heel free, for example, may require a check chain on the dog which is jerked momentarily before walking forward and the handler may hold his/her left hand on hip for the dog to be able to associate the fact that this is competitive heelwork – the command of 'heel' being of secondary importance. If the handler removes the chain or swings his left arm, even given the command of 'heel', the dog may not respond as effectively as when all of the associations are correct.

Or how about a dog trained to respond to the commands 'sit' 'stand' and 'down' either walking to heel or a short distance away from, and facing, the handler (distance control). Most people would believe that the dogs trained to carry out these exercises for competition really do understand the commands. Most dogs, however, have picked up a string of secondary associations along the way. So in distance control, for example, the handler 1) positions his dog behind a line (real or imaginary), and 2) sets his dog up for the exercise by placing it in any three positions, 3) walks away a number of paces and then 4) about turns to face the dog

and assumes a certain posture with his body. We already
have a set of four associations built into the exercise before
the first command is given to tell the dog which to adopt.
Suppose the dog has been left in the sit position and is
waiting for a command telling him which new position to
adopt; there are only two possible choices stand or down –
even a dog that doesn't fully understand the commands must
get it right half of the time. Let the same dog run in a field
and be playing with another dog and then command 'stand'
and, not surprisingly, most trainers get no reaction at all
from the dog. This system of training is referred to as 'pattern training' where a dog learns a pattern or a string of
associations without ever really fully understanding many
individual commands.

How about the retrieve. Do our dogs really understand
the command 'fetch'?. Think carefully about this one. The
dog is put into the sit position, given a command to remain
there, the article is thrown and the command 'fetch' is given.
Ninety-nine per cent of trained dogs would still retrieve if
the handler substituted the word 'rhubarb' for fetch. All of
the prior associations set the dog up for the act of retrieving;
the article being thrown is usually the primary association.
Place an article out of sight of the dog around the side of
a wall, then get the dog out of the car without making him
sit, sit on the floor yourself and command 'fetch'. You would
be lucky to get anything other than a puzzled expression
from your dog unless he understands the *command* and not
all of the other associations related to it.

It is also important that whichever commands are to be
trained, the dog should be trained to obey them the first
time it hears each of them. If I have the dog on a lead and
tell it to 'sit' four times before its bottom touches the floor,
I haven't taught it to sit on the fourth command, I have
taught it to disobey the first three. If I need to shout commands to get a response when the dog is alongside me then
I have no chance of getting a dog to obey me when it is two
hundred yards away.

Let us look at one of the commands in greater detail and
the right and wrong way of using our voice. An area of
difficulty a lot of beginners experience is teaching a dog to

hold something in its mouth. I've watched so many people making the same elementary mistakes it is a wonder that some trainers get a dog to hold at all!

The dog is placed in the sit position and its mouth is opened by pressing in its lips, just behind the canine teeth. As the retrieve article is placed in its mouth it is given the command 'hooooooold'. After a few seconds it manages to spit the article out and so the process is repeated. A few seconds later the article is spat out again, and this time it is placed in with a sharp command of '*hold*'. Out it comes again, and it is put back with a growled command of 'HOLD IT'. By now the poor dog has heard three completely different sounds made by its trainer, all of which it is supposed to interpret as meaning the same thing only by this time so much confusion and panic has set in that the dog is just not receptive to learning at all.

It is much easier for the dog to understand what is required if the command is *always* given in the same tone 'hooold'. If he makes a mistake and drops it we can growl '*no*' at him, but every time we put it in his mouth the command should sound the same, in other words I am not using the command 'hold' to punish him. Now it is starting to make a lot more sense, isn't it?

Reinforcement

As already stated, reinforcement can be either positive or negative and helps to promote the learning of the action that preceded it.

Let us take a look at the positive reinforcement and reward method of training.

There are several ways that we can reward progress and most of these fulfill a natural instinct in the dog.

These are as follows:

1. *Food.* All dogs can be trained to carry out commands in response to a tasty tidbit. A greedy dog will obviously respond more readily to this form of inducement, but even a dog which is not particular about working for food can be made

so simply by using all of it's daily food allowance when training.

2. *Water.* Although little used as an inducement, it is nevertheless quite effective provided the task that we are training our dog to perform is not long and arduous. Like food, water can be used in a similar manner but take care not to deprive a dog of water for an extended period, particularly in warm weather.

3. *Chase.* The instinct to chase a moving object is highly developed in some breeds of dogs and may be exploited as a method of reward. The most commonly used item is a ball which is thrown for the dog to chase and retrieve in order to motivate the dog to carry out the task that preceded it. Some dogs, however, have a poor chase instinct and in such cases little can be done to stimulate the dog to chase, which makes this method impractical for them.

4. *Kill.* This is an excellent system of reward as a great number of dogs enjoy 'killing' a piece of rag by gripping it with their teeth and shaking and pulling in a similar fashion to a dog actually making a kill. A rag or cloth or other article may be kept in the trainer's pocket, out of sight of the dog but ready to be produced for a game whenever a training association needs to be reinforced.

5. *Praise.* The most commonly used form of reward which exploits the dog's need for attention. This presupposes that the dog has some affection for its handler and it has been brought up to accept that being made a fuss of is a pleasant and earned experience. A dog that is stroked and petted constantly does not need to obey commands to be praised as this happens often enough in any case.

To improve the dog's response to praise, all that is necessary is to reserve most petting and stroking for training sessions. This ensures that during the session the dog will want to please and be with its owner.

6. *Reproduction.* The most basic instinct, but one that is not really practical to channel into training areas. A dogs desire to mate a bitch in season has been used occasionally to reinforce a dog's tracking capabilities, but to all intents and purposes we can virtually discount sex as a means of reward.

7. *Hunting.* Here we are looking at a dogs instinct, to use his nose to track down his quarry. This is not an easy instinct to make use of for practical training purposes. It is used more for working dogs who need to use this ability to track and search to find people or game.

8. *Possession.* More commonly referred to as tug-of-war. We can easily offer the dog a game with a rubber ring or the pull toy to improve response to a command we wish the dog to carry out when in close proximity to the handler, i.e., heel work.

How to make a reward more rewarding

A lot of owners actually diminish a dog's desire to work for a reward by over exposing the dog to the reward prior to carrying out a training session. Its no good expecting the dog to work for a ball if a ball is left lying around for him to play with whenever he wishes. By rationing the reward and only using it during training, the dog will work harder for it. The same applies to praise used as reward. If you come home from work and pat the dog on the head, then sit and watch the television for an hour and stroke the dog all of the time and then take him out and let him off the lead, why should he ignore the other dogs and come back to you on command? For the pat on the head? Of course not, he can get all he wants of that for doing nothing at home!

If I were going to train a dog to walk to heel for competition by using a ball as a reward, I would first get the ball out of the drawer where it is kept and then tease the dog for a few minutes with it without letting him get hold of it. I can now take him out and get him to work his heart out, just for a brief game with the ball that he so desperately wants. If I am going to offer a praise as reward I withhold *me* for an hour or so before a training session.

Practical use of positive reinforcement

All of the things that we want to train our dog to **want** to do are best attempted by using positive reinforcement methods.

1. The dog will enjoy the association with its training session.
2. A greater bond develops between dog and handler.
3. The dog will grow confidence
4. The dog should develop greater creativity.
5. The dog should work with a more positive attitude.
6. A poor trainer can do less damage to the dogs temperament and their relationship together if he uses positive reinforcement.

Let us now discuss this in greater detail. Because of the dog's enjoyment of receiving a reward (whatever the form that it may take), training becomes a pleasurable experience in some cases, more pleasurable than almost any other part of his daily or weekly routine. As the dog's training progresses, so the dog's trust in his handler increases and so the bond strengthens. As both handler and dog progress, each new task that the dog is being taught becomes quicker and easier. Even the most complex exercises can be mastered as this confidence increases.

When we talk about creativity in association with dogs, what we really mean is training the dog to become less inhibited by the constraints of the more complex exercises and encouraging him to be fairly flexible in his interpretation of a command or situation. I do not credit many dogs with an outstanding ability to think out a situation in order to reach a conclusion. Also, with positive training, we are encouraging the dog to work towards a purposeful outcome and thereby increase the dog's drive or motivation to carry out a command.

Some other points to consider regarding positive reinforcement training are;

1. It is generally slower to teach than negative methods.
2. In certain exercises we might think that creativity is the opposite of what we want from the dog.
3. It depends on the handlers ability to 'understand' his dog.
4. It requires a tremendous amount of self-control from the handler.
5. The reward needs to be made available during all training sessions.

Let us again discuss each of the above statements in greater detail.

Progress in positive training is usually slower than negative because the dog must learn to *want* the reward and the incentive used must be strong enough to carry the dog through the initial confusion that always surrounds the start of any new training exercise. In exercises such as down 'stay', we may not want the dog to expand and develop his knowledge of the exercise, we may simply want him to obey a command to the letter without giving a thought to any possible creative variations.

The handler needs to be very aware of his dog's requirements and must have the ability to 'turn the dog on' for work during a training session If at any stage, the dog's response starts to dwindle, the handler must be able to re-motivate his dog, to get him through bad patches.

The handler must also observe his dogs natural behaviour to be able to maintain the right balance between control and enthusiasm. Temper tantrums on the part of the handler are quite definitely out, with understanding and encouragement being the order of the day. Training sessions where the handler is in a bad mood can do untold damage at any stage in training.

Impromptu training sessions are *out* using the positive approach, as each session needs to be carefully planned to minimise the risk of the dog becoming bored by over rewarding. For example, it is no use using food as a reward and going out for a day's training with two pounds of cooked liver cut into pieces to reward the dog with at the completion of every exercise. After a certain period of time, which varies from dog to dog, the reward becomes not worth the effort of working for.

The overuse of reward method of reinforcing a training association will lessen the dog's (or for that matter, any other animal's) response to it.

It is easy to suppose that in order to increase the production in a factory, all one needs to do is make the rewards (financial) larger. For example, a man working as a bench fitter for forty hours per week might be taking home £100 per week. If we asked him to increase his work load and reward him by paying him twice his weekly wage i.e., £200 per week, sure enough, he would be more motivated due to the added incentive.

Let us now reward him even more by paying him £400 per week. Will he work harder still? At first, there is the possibility that he might, but after a while he starts to realise that he can afford to have time off work and has more money to spend on alternatives to work – leisure activities increase. In time he may have saved enough to retire early, start up his own business, or buy a share in someone else's. So the factory, far from making the worker more productive and conscientious, has actively encouraged him to be less so by over-rewarding him.

So once the dog has learned to obey a command using the smallest reward that will sustain the response, it must offered *every* time the dog carries out the correct action. By using a variety of rewards training becomes more exciting for the dog as he should not be able to anticipate *what* he is going to get, *when* he will get it or *how* much of it there will be.

The point at which the reward is given is also vital in maintaining the dog's interest or attention.

A person who smokes will often make use of a cigarette machine. Some coins are inserted and the reward (cigarettes) is predictably in the drawer when it is pulled. It is a habitual process which in itself is completely uninteresting once you have done it a few times. The only time when it is possibly more interesting is when a smoker is 'gasping for a cigarette'.

The same smoker may, however, stand for hours feeding coins into a one slot machine where the actions are similar but the reward becomes unpredictable.

Using heelwork as an example, let us suppose that we are going to make use of the dog's chasing instincts as a method of reward. After every fifty or so paces the handler halts, makes the dog sit, then rewards it by throwing the ball. Predictably, when several training sessions have elapsed, the dog's attention on its handler improves and it walks quite well at the heel, sitting in anticipation of the ball. because the reward becomes so predictable the dog may then start to lose interest in the actual walking to heel and become only interested in sitting at heel when the handler stops. The dog may also have the '*edge*' taken off his enthusiasm for the retrieving by repeatedly throwing the ball at shorter intervals in order to re motivate him.

Consider by using the same basic method to teach heel-work, only this time, when the dog has built up the correct association with the reward we will start to make things unpredictable. During a typical training session of five minutes, the reward may be thrown immediately after an about-turn, after a change of pace from fast to slow, after a right turn, during a long straight stretch of normal pace, after a left or left about-turn or after a halt. It is not always the ball that is thrown, the more toys that are used, the better the dog will maintain interest.

At an occasional session the ball will be thrown at the sit at heel before commencement of the exercise to prevent the dog anticipating the handler walking forward. Far from making the dog less interested he will now start to work as though his life depended on it. The 'gambling bug' will have started to take hold, for if the dog does not know at which point he is to be rewarded, or what he is going to get or how much of it there may be, he will usually pay more attention and work harder.

Negative reinforcement

More commonly known as avoidance learning or compulsion. Using negative reinforcement methods make use of a dog's natural instincts in order to compel it to carry out a command. These should always be used with descretion and **never** with harshness and cruelty.

1. *A disagreeable experience* This is the main agent of compulsion and can be applied in several different ways.
a) A check or choke chain tightening around the dog's throat causing varying degrees of discomfort which can be controlled by the handler/trainer.
b) A sharp slap given by the hand on the dog's rump, the severity of which is again controlled by the trainer.
c) Shaking the dog by the scruff of the neck, as it's mother would in order to discipline it.

2. *Voice and facial expression* If this method is used to reinforce training it is generally accomplished by use of the words **no** or **bad dog** until the dog assumes a submissive posture for any other than correct association.

3. *Fear.* Many dogs that have been subjected to an unpleasant experience in early life will retain this fear which may be associated with certain sounds, sights or smells. For example, a dog that was frightened as a young puppy by the sound of gunfire might retain it's fear of sudden loud noises.

3. *Solitary confinement.* Very occasionally trainers try to make negative use of a dog's desire for companionship by 'locking it away' as a punishment for performances in training. This method, unless under expert supervision is usually unsuccessful.

Practical use of negative reinforcement

Let us now have a look at training using negative reinforcement methods.

1. Negative training can be quicker for the dog to learn than reward based methods.
2. It tends to produce stereotyped behaviour.
3. Little knowledge of canine instinct or behaviour is required.
4. Any dog lacking in enthusiasm may be trained using negative methods for control exercises.
5. A handler lacking in self-control would adapt easier to negative training (though I would never recommend anyone who is short of patience to even own a dog).
6. Negative training is retained for a greater length of time than positive training with less maintenance being required.

If the dog is subjected to an unpleasant experience, in a very short space of time he may try to avoid that experience by carrying out his trainers wishes.

In some cases, particularly for some competitive exercises the stereotyped behaviour that avoidance learning procedures may be seen to be highly desirable, for example the retrieve of a dumbbell where the dog is required to pick up cleanly without pouncing or rolling the dumbbell, hold it without mouthing, return to its handler, sit straight in front with the dumbbell close to the handler until it is taken.

Another example is distance control where the dog is required to execute three different positions, namely the sit, stand and down at a distance from its handler, without forward movement.

Using negative methods, a handler can be successful without ever needing to fully understand his dog. This of course, is dependent on the training instructor's ability to coach his pupil to apply 'correction' at the right moment. The dog then sometimes becomes merely a tool which the handler uses in order to carry out his trade.

It is quite often easier to use negative methods on a dog which is quite difficult to motivate rather than spend lots of time in trying to find things which may 'turn the dog on'. A number of 'hard' dogs are frequently trained using compulsion-the dog's ability to bounce back after correction being a desirable attribute with some trainers.

There are occasions where negative methods, once applied, will last for the dog's lifetime. As an example of this it is possible to train a dog not to steal food from a table by catching him in the act and subjecting him to a sudden disagreeable experience. If the dog associates the disagreeable experience with the act of stealing, he will probably never try to steal from that table ever again *in the presence of the person who was responsible for causing the unpleasantness*. This is known as *passive avoidance learning*, the dog learns *not* to do something to avoid the unpleasant experience.

The other type of avoidance learning is known as *active avoidance learning* where the dog learns *to do* something to avoid the disagreeable experience. An example might be a dog being trained to hold a dumbell and the trainer smacking him every time that the dumbell is dropped. The dog then learns to hold (do something) to avoid the unpleasantness.

Some of the disadvantages of negative training methods are as follows:

1. It is inflexible and difficult to extinguish.
2. Mistakes are difficult to correct.
3. It lacks creativity.
4. Dog's (and handler's) enjoyment of training diminishes.
5. It can be injurious to both dog and handler.
6. Applied incorrectly it can trigger off aggressive tendencies in the dog.

We will now examine these points in greater detail.

Consider a dog which has been trained to drop (lie down) to a whistle by teaching it that when it hears the whistle the only way to avoid an unpleasant pleasant experience is to drop very quickly. At this stage I will not go into how that is achieved, but let us assume that the dog has learned its lesson well. If we suddenly decide we now want the dog to sit instead of drop, on hearing the whistle, imagine the difficulties involved. Because of the dog's past associations with the whistle, each attempt to retrain the dog to sit would generally result in reinforcing the down position. By causing this confusion the dog is even more likely to remember its past associations with the command and drop. It becomes even more difficult to teach the dog to disregard the whistle completely, as he will never wait to see if the compulsion will be applied but will drop as a means of avoiding the anticipated punishment for not carrying out the command.

Lack of creativity in some exercises may not necessarily be a disadvantage, but in many areas of training there is a definite advantage to be gained in exploiting the dog's creativity. Too much negative training, especially early in the dog's life, will suppress the dog's ability to adjust and adapt to situations he may meet in every day life or in competitions but which he has never met in training. A good example would be to imagine a dog trained totally using negative reinforcement to carry out distance control in an obedience ring. Putting the same dog in the back of an unfamiliar estate car and then seating the handler on a deck chair ten or so paces away, we would find that even though the commands are the same, the dog would act as though he had never been trained to carry out the exercise. He finds it difficult to adapt and would either adopt a submissive posture or panic out of confusion. A positively reinforced dog might adopt a trial-and-error approach in anticipation of his reward.

Because of the physical and mental demands made on the dog and handler, training sessions tend to be frustrating affairs, with the dog showing obvious relief at the conclusion of each trained exercise. Some people might misinterpret this as the dog's enjoyment of working to a successful conclusion but let me pose the following question. Have you ever seen a dog performing agility tests? Most handlers in this increasingly popular sport would admit that their dogs get very excited at the prospect of working, to the extent that they are reluctant to have to come away from the jumps after their "round". I have witnessed several dogs, whilst waiting their turn to go on, that have managed to break free of their handlers and have started the course by themselves just for the fun of it. It is, however, very rare to see a dog getting excited about the prospect of entering an obedience ring, or being reluctant to leave after the completion of its work.

Handlers using the negative approach usually get little or no enjoyment from the actual training sessions but tend to see them as a necessary evil. "I must go out and train tonight as there is a competition next weekend" is an expression that will be familiar with far too many handlers.

Apart from the obvious hazard of injuring the dog (or handler) by a badly directed or mistimed smack, there are other less obvious problems that may occur. I have had many dogs to train that have had poor hips (hip displasia). This is a fact that the owners may not have been aware of and considerable pain and suffering could have been caused by them insisting that the dog sat quickly and upright when they halted during heelwork. There are many other physical problems that can be aggravated by compulsion training.

With some of the more nervous or insecure dogs, a frequent occurrence is that negative methods trigger off nervous aggression or fear biting. When a dog knows, by association, that he is to be punished, he will always have three choices. One is to accept the punishment. The second choice is to run. The third choice is to prepare and defend himself and get the first bite in. If I were to pick out one breed of dog on which negative methods are nearly always unsuccessful it would be the Dobermann. These dogs have an undeserved reputation of being hard, dominant dogs and to be mastered at all costs. The result? More Dobermann owners get bitten by their own dogs than owners of most other breeds.

Summary

If we want to train the dog to want to do anything we should always first try positive reinforcement and reward methods.

If we want to train the dog not to carry out a particular action (bite the postman, steal food, jump up on furniture, etc.) negative methods can be considered.

Here is a table which shows the most likely methods a beginner would use to train the various exercises ten years ago.

Exercise	Positive	Negative
Heel on lead		*
Heel free		*
Recall	*	
Retrieve		*
Sit, down & stand stay		*
Sendaway (Obedience)		*
Sendaway (Trials)	*	
Scent		*
Distance Control		*
Steadiness to gunshot	*	
Track	*	
Search (articles)	*	
Speak on command	*	
Agility	*	

Compare this with how the same exercises are usually taught, with more success today.

Exercise	Positive	Negative
Heel on lead	*	
Heel free	*	
Recall	*	
Retrieve		*
Sit, down & stand stay	*	
Sendaway (Obedience)	*	
Sendaway (Trials)	*	
Scent	*	
Distance Control	*	
Steadiness to gunshot	*	
Track	*	
Search (articles)	*	
Speak on command	*	
Agility	*	

As you can see it is only the retrieve exercise that still seems to be persistently trained using negative reinforcement and punishment techniques, particularly in America. This is sad because in most cases the retrieve is very easy to train without resorting to the more negative techniques.

An experienced trainer would always start training every exercise by using a system of reward and only consider using a very small amount of compulsion should the reward system fail.

I must reiterate that negative reinforcement methods should never never be used in temper or with harshness. The trainer must think very carefully about the degree of severity applied. There is never any reason or excuse for cruelty. Positive reinforcement builds a bond between dog and handler. Negative reinforcement can easily break down the bond.

4

Companion and Competition training

Control exercises

It should be noted that there are no right and wrong ways of training each of the following exercises, It is up to you, the trainer to use or adapt one of the "methods" to suit yourself and your individual dog. I have listed both positive and negative reinforcement methods on each exercise, and have also made a distinction between pet and competition training which may prove useful to the prospective trainer. I should point out that once a dog has been trained to carry out the "pet" version of most exercises, it will need to be retrained and maintained at a higher level of reinforcement if the owner subsequently decides to train for competition.

Recall

One of the most important of all exercises for either pet or competitive purposes and the easiest one to train out of all the exercises listed. It is also one of the most misinterpreted exercises by both owners and dogs! The command "come" or "here", etc, should mean, "Whatever you are doing, come back to me immediately." Simple, isn't it? So how can we achieve that? First of all you should examine the relationship between you and your dog. How much does your dog want either you or the "reward" that you have in your pocket? A dog that is off the lead and running free (as opposed to being left in a "stay" position) can only be trained to come back because it wants to, and there are several ways to achieve this.

Let us imagine that we have a young puppy that already understands his name and the command which tells him that there is something pleasant in store for him if he runs towards the person giving the command. He is now over his injections and able to go out into the big outside world to exercise. We have unclipped his lead and let him off in a big, enclosed field and watch him venture further away. After a few minutes we decide to call him back.

Method a) Hide and Seek. When the puppy is preoccupied with exploring and is unaware of movement on your part, run and hide downwind of the dog. When he realizes he has lost you, panic will start to set in and he will rush about blindly trying to find you. After several minutes of this panic, call his name with his recall command as you come out of your hiding place. When the pup gets to you, reward him with food, a game with a toy and/or really make a fuss of him. Then let him continue his exercise and call him back two or three times more to check his response.

If you have put the correct association in his mind he shouldn't ever let you out of his sight again whilst exercising as he will have "losing you" imprinted for life.

Method b) Run Away. When the pup is exercising, try calling his name with a command and running away from him at the same time. After several yards, let him catch you up and reward him as above. The effect is similar to hide and seek. As the pup hears his name and turns to look, he sees you disappearing and feeling insecure will rush to join you, completely forgetting the nice smell he was preoccupied in sniffing when you called. Repeat the process several times at each exercise session.

Method c) Cord. When you take the lead off to allow your dog to exercise free attach a ten yard length of fine nylon line to his collar. Let him pull the line behind him, but do not hold on to it. Several times during the exercise session pick up the end of the line, call the pup's name with your chosen command and give the line a really sharp tug. Immediately drop the line as the pup turns around, then use whatever means available to encourage the pup to return. It is vital that the pup does not connect the "shock" with you. It is useless to tug on the line if the dog is facing you. That way he will probably connect that the cord is associated with you holding the end of it and although he will return on command when the line is attached, as soon as it is removed his response to the command goes with it.

Even though the dog may return without problems when just its owner is with it there is bound to come a time when it is distracted by another dog, person, rabbit, etc., and ignores the command to return. When this happens and the dog does eventually return to you, push him away and be really cool and rejecting. Show the dog all of the rewards that he could have had but let him have none of them. Walk away from him until he tries harder to please you and then repeat the recall a second time. This time reward him well when he obeys. If all else fails then take out all of your dogs food and feed him portions of it every time he responds to coming when called. If this is the only food that he is allowed to eat for two weeks then you will usually have a good recall by the end of that time. If you consider trying a negative reinforcement method once you are sure that your dog understands the recall command then you can ask someone to accompany you to the exercise area and get them to try throwing a plastic lemonade bottle, with a few pieces of gravel inside, towards the dog everytime that he disobeys a command to return. The "shock" is usually sufficient to make him return and look to you for comfort. If you are then down on one knee and calling in a nice pleasant tone to reassure him, the chances are that he will want to return because of the disturbance associated with the other dog, person, rabbit, etc. Of course, he mustn't connect the plastic bottle landing with you otherwise he will stray further away, so he must not see *you* throw it. Your command will then, hopefully, get him to return instantly to avoid the "shock" that the command warns him of. Reward lavishly each and every time he returns.

If your dog already has problems on the recall then we first need to isolate their cause before things can improve.

Recall problems can be divided into three main categories, and in order to improve your dog's response to a command to return it is first necessary to find out which of the three problems you have.

1. When off the lead, the dog will not actually run away but will keep you in sight, ignoring any commands to come back until he has either
   a) finished exercising and will reluctantly allow you to put the lead on, or
   b) until you manage to sneak up on him whilst he is preoccupied with sniffing, etc.

2. When off the lead, the dog will actually come near you when called but will stop about five yards or so away in the head-down attitude. The slightest movement towards the dog and it rushes away again, until either you sneak up on him or he finishes his exercise.

3. When off the lead, the dog will run away and maintain a considerable distance between himself and you. Walking towards the dog would tend to make him move further away, walking away from the dog would generally make him come much closer. Sometimes the dog returns home by himself ahead of you; sometimes he will follow you home. Only rarely will you be able to catch him to put the lead on.

Before we attempt to solve each problem, let us have a look at the cause.

First of all, dogs are a product of their upbringing and environment and so, like it or not, your dog's failure to come when called is due to you having trained it not to come when called.

If your dogs falls into category 1 it is a fair bet that you have other training problems, i.e., will not stay when told, will not walk properly to heel on the lead, etc. This usually occurs when the dog passes through puppyhood without any formal training, or because owners expect their dogs to understand what is required without training the required response.

For the next couple of weeks, when you exercise your dog attach a fifteen yard line to his collar in place of the lead (a light washing line will do for this). Let him drag the line around for ten minutes or so until he gets used to the feel of it. Do not hold onto the end of the line, as your dog must not "think" that you are in control. Then, whenever your dog is preoccupied with sniffing, etc, pick up the end of the line without him seeing, give him a command ("Fido here" or "Fido come") and at the same moment give a really sharp jerk on the line, then dropping it immediately and praising him well as he returns. If he stops on the way back repeat the command and the jerk – do not pull him in. Each day, as his response to the command improves, cut off a yard of the line until the line has gone completely but the response to the command remains.

If your dog falls into category 2 it is likely that in its youth it has been grabbed by the scruff of the neck or the collar whenever it came near enough and was then promptly put on the lead and taken home. It may also have been chased and grabbed in the house whenever it was misbehaving.

To remedy this behaviour will take a lot of patience on your part. Every time you exercise your dog, instead of taking the lead off, simply leave go of the end. After a couple of minutes call your dog back. Stand up straight, putting your hands behind your back and using your voice in an encouraging manner. If your dog stops short of you, take a couple of paces backwards, again encouraging the dog to come closer. (This may well take quite a while.) As soon as your dog is close enough put one foot on the end of his lead to prevent him moving away, bring your hands forward and stroke him. Really let him know that he has done well. Then stand up and release him to run free again. Repeat the process at least ten times at each exercise session to get the message across that to come back when called does not usually meant that the dog has to go home immediately.

If your dogs falls into category 3 it is likely that on one or more occasions when the dog has failed to respond to a command to come back, you have caught him and chastised him (usually by striking him with the lead). Your dog will now not come back because he associated your recall command with some form of punishment.

This is the most difficult recall problem to put right as it depends on someone being able to break down the dog's previous associations with the command. This is usually easier to do if someone other than the owner does the necessary training. Much can be done in the house by offering tidbits as an inducement to come from one room to the next, etc., for a couple of weeks or so. Then you should withhold all food for twelve hours, after which you must allow your dog to watch you make his usual meal. Put the dish with the food into a carrier bag and take him out for exercise. Let him off the lead putting the lead in your pocket out of sight. The chances are that he will not go too far away as he knows you have his dinner. At any convenient point, when your dog is several yards away and not looking at you, call him in holding his bowl as an inducement. Let him eat a small amount and then lift up the bowl and repeat. After several such sessions on successive evenings (the only way he is getting fed), substitute dog treats or liver pieces for the bowl of food and give him his main meal after returning from an exercise session never before one.

All of the above training would normally be carried out initially without the distracting influence of other people/dogs etc., until the response is correct.

Failure to come when called due to aggression with other dogs/people would be classed as behaviour rather than training.

Walking to heel

Training a dog to walk correctly by the handler's side without pulling starts from the moment a collar and lead are put on the pup's neck for the first time. Assuming that the pup is used to wearing a collar, the next step is to attach a flat nylon lead and let him get used to the feel of this by allowing him to drag it around the house for a half hour or so for two or three consecutive days. Then attach the lead and spend twenty minutes or so simply walking your dog from one room to the other and out into the garden and back.

During this "walk" the pup should be coaxed and encouraged as much as possible, although there will be times when the pup is apprehensive and tries to fight against the pressure of the lead. When this happens try not to exert sustained pressure on the lead, but try to make the pup go where you want by using a series of gentle pulls on the lead. As soon as the pup begins to walk in the direction that you want, use as much praise and encouragement as possible. If the pup puts the brakes on and sits, just keep walking and say nothing. Praise lavishly when he begins to walk with you. The same thing applies if he rears up like a wild horse. Until you can get him to walk happily on the lead in the house and garden for a few minutes several times a day it is pointless taking him outside.

It usually helps a great deal if you simply get your dog used to being fastened up on a short lead whilst you groom it every day. If it struggles against the pressure of the lead, keep grooming it but stop speaking. As soon as the dog relaxes the pressure that it is exerting on the lead then praise lavishly with your voice. When a dog will accept being fastened on a short lead it becomes generally easier to walk on a slack lead.

The first time you take the dog out for a walk outside the house do so before one of his mealtimes and carry a few tasty treats in your pocket. Try, whenever possible, to choose a quiet route for the first few excursions and walk the pup in the centre of the pavement to discourage him from sniffing at walls, gates, doorways, etc. Dogs are traditionally walked on the handler's left, but only becomes necessity if any form of competition is contemplated later.

Method 1. If the pup tries to dash forwards, stand still and give a sharp tug on the lead, sufficient to stop the pup dead in its tracks and make it stand upright without leaning on the lead. Then, keeping the lead slack, praise verbally *for at least ten seconds* before walking forward again. If you carry this out correctly the dog should feel a sudden tug via the lead and collar which lasts only for a fraction of a second. Do not pull the pup backwards on the lead. The correct technique is to snap the lead tight and instantly release it. For every twenty yards that the pup walks without exerting any pressure on the lead reward it by stopping and giving a tidbit. With some of the toy breeds it is worth carrying the pup several hundred yards away from the house and walking the pup back to the house to overcome any apprehension it may show on leaving its home. If you take your dog along the same route to the local park each day it will start to get excited and be more inclined to pull in anticipation of its exercise session. If this happens, each time that the lead tightens because of the dog forging ahead, snap the lead tight as above and then go back twenty yards before walking forwards again. The idea is that if the dog pulls to gain his "reward" quicker, he finds himself farther away from his destination. It is always best to take the lead off in the local park in different places so that the dog does not anticipate that once inside the gates he is free to run.

Method 2. If the pup continually forges ahead even though the lead and collar have been used correctly as above, try doing an about-turn as the lead snaps to check the dog's forward progress and continue walking in the opposite direction until the lead starts to tighten again. Repeat as often as necessary but be sure to reward well for every twenty yards that the dog walks without exerting any pressure on the lead.

You will notice that we have not used the command "heel" or "walkies" at all because we are trying to teach the dog to adopt a position "at heel" we are teaching him not to pull on the lead. The two things are not connected. If you want to teach your dog to obey the command heel, then read the section on competition exercises, page 118. The lead being clipped to your dog's collar should be its incentive to walk without pulling, not your command. I know that nearly all dog-training clubs try to instruct the handlers to use the command heel when they trudge round and round the dog club hall where the dogs are not going anywhere but round and round. After several weeks that's all the dogs are conditioned to do, walk around the hall on the command heel. They still pull when outside because they have never been trained otherwise.

When we talk about dogs pulling on the lead we are really talking about three problems, the dog that has been a) trained to pull against the pressure of the lead on its neck, b) allowed to dictate to its owner where it wants to walk or c) trained to brace itself and then pull on the command "heel". The first problem is by far the most common and

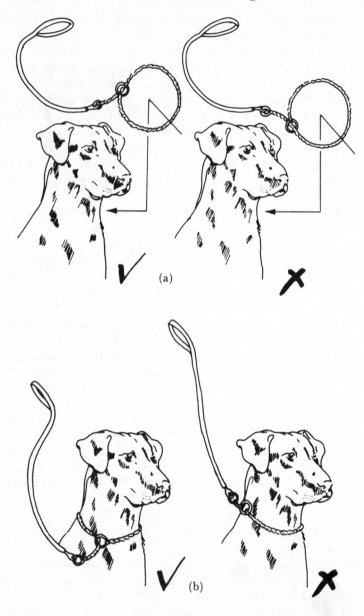

(a)

(b)

Figure 1 *The right and wrong ways to put on the check chain*

is caused by the incorrect lead selection and/or technique in using it on a puppy. When the pup is taken out for the first time the lead has been kept tight on the dog so that it can be "guided" where the owner wants it to walk. Because of the sustained pressure on the dog's neck, its muscles in this area and in its hind legs start to develop. As it grows and the muscles become stronger the pulling gets progressively worse. A check chain is then put on in the belief that the pressure of the chain tightening and choking the dog will teach it to walk to heel. It won't of course. It will only make the dog emit choking noises as it pulls harder and harder.

Dogs in category b) are easily spotted because they not only pull in front of the owner but also and more often pull to the side, away from their owner. That is because, in early life, the owner has allowed the pup to pull towards and sniff at lampposts, garden gates grass verges, etc. As the pup grows it learns that by putting pressure on the lead in the direction that it want to go, the owner will allow it to reach these otherwise inaccessible places. The owner's arm then starts to become an extension of the range of the lead. To cure the problem buy a lead and chain as in a) but begin by holding it fairly tight so that the dog is encouraged to lean away from you towards lampposts, etc. When the dog is leaning against the lead suddenly, and without prior warning, take a pace towards the dog so that the lead momentarily slackens. The dog will now be caught off balance so now you can immediately snap the lead tight, using sufficient force to bring the dog's progress to an abrupt halt. The direction of checking should be directly opposite to the direction that the dog was pulling. Keep the lead slack for several yards until the dog feels brave enough to start leaning on the lead again and repeat as often as is necessary. If you haven't succeeded within ten minutes you haven't made it rewarding enough for the dog to want to be with you. It cannot be emphasized too strongly that when the dog is walking as you wish, his reward should be to think that he is the best dog that's ever been born. To say "praise him well" is an understatement.

How about the dog that's been trained to brace itself and pull on the command "heel". The word is repeated every few steps along the road and as soon as the command is given, the dog braces itself for the check it is expecting then continues to pull in front until it hears the warning command again.

Try to see things from the dog's point of view. If I put the chain on you and each time you moved in front of me I bellowed "heel" and then tried to pull your head off, would you want to walk near to me or further away? In other words if you saw me as being the cause of an unpleasant experience would you not want to pull away from me the same as your dog does? The trick in using a lead correctly is to use it to make the dog walk in a balanced and upright fashion so that you can reward it when it is correct. If we now take the dog for a walk and forget about bellowing and shouting "heel", but instead without any warning whatsoever snap the lead tight and reward as in b) the dog cannot brace himself and will therefore get a shock that is in no way connected with its owner who is now the most pleasant person to walk next to!

For dogs that pull on the lead to bark or lunge at other people see "Aggression" in Chapter 2, page 62.

Sit stay, stand stay, down stay

All of the above exercises are useful for the pet dog and are dealt with in detail under the section on competition training. An important point to make is that whenever a dog is left in a stay position outside a shop or anywhere near a public highway, no matter how well trained it is the lead should be fastened to any convenient point to prevent the dog from wandering away. You may well be able to guarantee your dog's trained response to a command, but you cannot anticipate the behaviour of any "stray" dog that may come along and possibly intimidate him into moving onto the road.

Retrieve

To start the retrieve we must first presuppose that the correct games have been played with the puppy to encourage the development of its chase instinct (see "Toys" page 24). If your dog shows little or no desire to run after anything that you throw you will need to read the competition section of this book. Another important thing is to have a good, free-running recall as opposed to the more formal competition recall.

So let us start our training process and the best retrieve article to start with is a piece of rolled-up carpet about one inch in diameter and about six inches long.

Method 1. Take the dog into a quiet area with as few distractions as possible. Remove the retrieve article from your pocket and tease your dog with it for several minutes both by dragging it along the ground for the dog to chase without letting him catch it and by throwing it into the air and catching it yourself. When the dog is sufficiently interested, keep him on the lead and throw the article several yards away,, giving the dog's name and the command "fetch", As soon as he picks the article up, walk backwards and call the dog to you using your lead and recall command. Continue walking backwards until the dog is close to you. Then stand still, gently make a fuss of him *without removing the article from his mouth*. Continue rewarding him with your voice and stroking him with your hands for at least twenty seconds before taking the article. When you take the article, stop praising him because it is important that he associates the praise with holding and not releasing. If you offer praise after you have taken the article, your dog may well start to drop the article, instead of delivering it to hand, anticipating the praise he gets for releasing rather than for holding it.

If it is dropped short of you then quickly walk forward and kick the article away to re-motivate the dog.

If the dog brings the article to you and spits it out when your hands go down to take it, continue walking backwards encouraging the dog to pick it up again. As the dog's response improves you can slowly reduce the amount of movement away from the dog after he has picked the article up.

Never leave the article around for him to play with. It must only be used for training. When you get to the stage where the mere sight of the article excites the dog you can dispense with the lead and either let him run straight out for it, or make him stay until he hears the command "fetch". If you then want to progress to different retrieve articles, the best way is to wrap the piece of carpet around anything that you want your dog to retrieve, removing it only when he understands what is required.

Method 2. Excite the dog as above and throw the article. As it lands, run out with the dog on the lead. If he picks it up then praise well then back away as above. If he drops it or loses interest when he gets to the article, snatch it up yourself and have a game with it. Your dog may soon learn to try and pick it up before you do, and when that happens it is important to praise well and use the lead to coax and encourage the dog to bring it to you by backing away as in method 1.

When the dog is responding to your command correctly on the lead you can, first of all, let go of the lead and let him run out and back with the lead trailing. The lead is picked up and used only if the dog appears reluctant to return. You can then dispense with the lead when the dog is happily retrieving to your satisfaction.

When you first try the retrieve when there are other distractions to take the dog's attention you should go back to teasing him with the article before you throw it, and even then only throw it a very short distance.

Retrieve problems are dealt with in full under the competition section.

Creative exercises

Finding a lost article

This is an extremely useful and enjoyable extension of the retrieve exercise which allows the dog a degree of mental as well as physical exercise. Assuming that we have a good enthusiastic retrieve on the article we want the dog to find, ball, slipper, car keys, purse, etc., we can start teaching him to use his nose to locate the article when we have hidden it. I will describe the exercise trained both inside the house and outside, at the local park, etc. as there are a few differences between the methods.

Inside the house start by throwing the retrieve article behind some obstacle such as a magazine rack. As soon as it disappears out of sight release the dog with a command of "find", "seek" or "lost", the choice is yours. As soon as he gets close to the article, reward him gently with an encouraging "good boy". When he gets to it you can tell him to "fetch" to get him to pick up and retrieve. For the first sessions he will only be using visual memory and not his nose in response to your command. At the next training session choose a different obstacle in the same room to throw the article behind, such as a coffee table tipped onto its side, the important point being that from where the dog is sent he must not be able to see the article. Repeat as for the first training session. At the third session, tease him with the article and then throw it behind either of the two obstacles you have used for the first two sessions. Release the dog with your chosen command, encouraging him if he chooses the correct location and remaining silent if he chooses the wrong location.If he starts to look puzzled and loses interest, take him and show him where the article is but do not let him get it. Pick it up yourself and tease him before repeating the exercise. He must only achieve his "reward" if he finds it. In a short space of time you should be able to throw the article behind either obstacle at random without the dog seeing and then send him to find it in the knowledge that if he fails to find it at the first place he checks, he will move to the second location, find and retrieve it.

You can now introduce a third and fourth location, and then start to lengthen the time interval between throwing the article and sending the dog on command. When you get to the point where you can throw the article with the dog's eyes hidden and wait for a minute before releasing him to race around to find and retrieve it you can start to eliminate eyesight and memory and encourage the dog to work using its scenting capacity. To do this have the dog positioned outside the open door of the room you are using. Tease the dog with the article then go into the room closing the door behind you (leaving the dog outside) and hide the article. Return to the dog and use your command to send the dog into the room to find and retrieve. Then try hiding the article in the room and going away for a short time before returning to the room, opening the door and sending the dog to find. You can now start to hide the article underneath objects where the dog cannot see it at all. An upside-down plastic pot is good for starters. The dog will be able to smell where the article is hidden, but not see it at all. You may need to tip the pot over yourself at first to help the dog recover the article. You can then hide the article under the edge of a rug, under a book, behind a cushion etc., as the dog's concentration improves. Then repeat the exercise in every room of the house.

The end result should be that when you show your dog the article and then go and hide it (or get someone else to) anywhere in the house, when you give your dog its command to find it should check every room in turn until it finds the article and returns it to you. It should be noted that when anyone outside the immediate family is asked to hide the article they should avoid handling it as much as possible otherwise their own characteristic smell may well mask the more familiar smell of the article. If at any point your dog fails to find the article, show him where it was hidden but do not let him get it. Tease him with it and repeat the exercise again. Always reward success.

Training your dog to find a "lost" article outside is a little different because we need to take wind direction and terrain into account. We can then define the exercise as a search "square" because we are going to teach the dog to restrict the area of his movements to approximately twenty-five yards square in front of and upwind of its handler.

Start by pushing a couple of bamboo canes about five yards apart and about ten yards upwind of where you are going to send your dog from. The grass must be sufficiently long to prevent the dog from seeing the article until he gets to within a yard of it. Throw the article so that it lands somewhere between the canes. This will aid the dog in locating the article. Wait a few seconds and then send the dog to "find" using your chosen command. When he gets near it

Sit, stay. Note how the lead is held to keep the dog in the correct position

Giant Schnauzer negotiating a six foot high scale jump

Any dog can be trained to retrieve. The sit and hold forms an important stage in this training

Collie clearing a 3-foot hurdle to maintain maximum speed. Compare that with the other Collie on the same jump (*opposite*) this time jumping to obtain maximum clearance. The techniques required for agility and working trials are not the same

Tracking on a harness and line. Note how the dog pulls into its harness enabling the handler to 'feel', from the tension, whether the dog is tracking or not

Competition heelwork training bears little or no resemblance to teaching a dog to walk without pulling on the lead

praise gently with a quiet "good boy". As he picks the article up, call him in and praise well. If he races past the canes, call him back using your recall command, show him the article but do not let him touch it, tease him and repeat. This also applies if he fails to find it and starts to lose interest. At the end of the first session, with the canes to guide him and the wind blowing the scent off the article towards him, he should have little difficulty in finding and retrieving it.

At the second session, after throwing the article, turn the dog around two or three times to disorientate him. He should still remember that you have thrown the article but will not have been able to "mark" the spot where it landed. When he is released with his find command it will take him longer to locate it because he has to use his nose more than his visual memory. Gently encourage him to "fetch" it if you think that the dog has located the smell of the article "on the wind". Praise him well when he returns with it and have a game of retrieve or tug-of-war before repeating a few times more.

At the next session you can start increasing the distance between the poles and also the distance from you to the poles in stages up to about twenty-five yards. The article is still thrown anywhere between the two poles, and the time lag between throwing the article and the dog being sent increased in stages up to about a minute or so. The next stage is to throw the article in, unseen by the dog who is fastened out of sight behind a hedge, fence, etc, bringing the dog up and give him his command to find. As he works into the wind, use as little encouragement as necessary to allow him to concentrate on his task. Reward well when he finds and retrieves. If he fails to locate at any stage, take him up and show the article but do not let him touch it. Tease him and then repeat. With a pet dog you can then remove first one then both bamboo canes as his response to your command improves. He should be conditioned to move away about twenty-five yards, and move right and left using the wind to locate the article.

Let us now suppose that you place the article, out of sight of the dog, only ten yards away from where you are going to send your dog from. On command he may well run past it and start searching twenty-five yards away. By slowly walking backwards fifteen yards your dog will start to adjust his position in relation to you until he is in a position to wind-scent the article. By moving forward he should move forwards to maintain approximately twenty-five yards between himself and you. Move right and you should get a corresponding movement in your dog. The same should work if you move left. If you make the search area particularly difficult and it takes your dog several minutes to find the article, as he tires both mentally and physically he will slowly search nearer to where you are standing and be less inclined to search at a distance. That is why it is policy to teach the dog to search at a distance first and then as he tires allow him to come closer to search. You can't do things the other way around. As your dog gets better at searching, you can drop the article into long grass at the start of an exercise session and on completion of his exercise position him downwind by about twenty-five yards and send him to find. You can also have a friend to hide the article in long grass, but make sure that they do not over handle the article thereby masking its familiar scent. You will notice that we have thrown the article so that the only way that the dog can find it is by wind scenting. If you walk out and place the article, the dog may learn to find it by tracking your footsteps.

If you want to progress further with this exercise then read the search exercise under competition training, page 161.

Tracking to find a lost person

Tracking to find lost articles is dealt with under the competition heading, but amongst pet dogs the exercise of tracking to find a person is easier and just as enjoyable for the dog and owners than the more demanding competitive tracking. To teach your dog to track for a person you will need a special tracking "harness" and a length of line, preferably soft climbing rope, with a good clip fastened on one end. The line needs to be about ten yards in length. The harness can be purchased or home made and figure 2 should enable anyone who is reasonably good with their hands to make a serviceable piece of equipment. The requirements for training a pet dog to track to find a person are as follows:

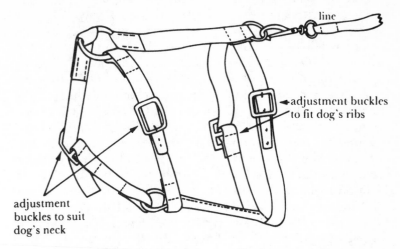

Figure 2   *Pattern for a tracking harness*

1. The "missing" person must be well known to the dog, preferably a member of the dog's immediate family.
2. The "missing" person must carry something to reward the dog for finding him, such as food or the dog's favourite toy.
3. Early training tracks are best done on grassland that has been undisturbed by people or animals for at least twenty-four hours.
4. We are going to teach the dog to track using a combination of wind and ground scent and so if you are even remotely interested in competition training ignore the following pages and read competition tracking.
5. The dog must be reasonably fit and training should never be attempted if the dog has eaten a meal during the four hours preceding a session.
6. You will need several bamboo canes.
7. Weather conditions can affect the dog's ability to track, but if we are only going to train our dog to track on grass and on a track not older than about half an hour, that is time elapsed from the "missing" person walking away to the dog being put on the track, we need not worry too much about the weather.

Start by placing the harness on the dog, attach the line and get a friend to hold onto the line quite firmly. Whatever reward you are going to use, tease the dog with it and then walk backwards directly into the wind shuffling your feet as you go in order to leave a continuous line of scent on the grass. Continue for about seventy yards or so, calling the dog by name and holding the reward out as you go. The more you excite and motivate the dog the better; don't worry if he is screaming to get to you. Then duck out of sight behind any convenient natural obstacle such as a tree, hedge, etc. After several seconds, get your friend to walk forward at a fairly fast pace and allow the dog to pull on ahead about halfway along the length of line (a knot placed halfway along will help); the remainder of the line is left trailing behind the handler. A command can be used if you so wish, but the usual association with tracking is simply to have the harness put on. The tracking harness is used only for this specific purpose. As soon as your dog reaches you, reward him by throwing the ball, offering food, etc. Repeat twice more at this session, using a different strip of land for each track. As with the search exercise the dog is reaching his "reward" by using his eyesight rather than his nose the first few times, but then through training we are going to slowly eliminate sight and memory and teach him to track a line of scent.

At the next session get a friend to hold the dog on the harness and line while you tease it with the "reward". The dog must be positioned behind any kind of visual barrier so that when you walk away, within twenty yards you are out of sight of the dog. As soon as you are out of sight, push a bamboo cane into the ground then continue for another hundred yards or so, walking directly into the wind. Just before you hide behind a bush, push a second bamboo cane into the ground. The person holding the dog should wait for a minute or so and then walk him forward. The handler will see the line you have taken because there are two bamboo canes to guide him. The dog, having been unable to see the direction that you walked will not be able to use his visual memory at all and will only be able to find you using his sense of smell. He should be encouraged to move forward by the handler who should walk in a straight line between the canes. The dog's movement away from the line of track is restricted by the length of line. If the dog moves more than two or three yards away from the track you have walked then the handler must stand still until the dog is pulling in the correct direction. When the dog finds you reward well and repeat another couple of times.

After another couple of training sessions you can ask your friend to hide, teasing the dog with the reward before walking away, out of sight to hide. Once again, if bamboo canes are used to indicate the line of track, you should be able to help your dog by preventing him from making mistakes. Get the missing person to reward the dog when he finds him. Up to now the dog is finding his reward by a combination of wind and track scent. To eliminate wind scenting, you can then start laying your track and hiding downwind of the dog. The only way that the dog can find the missing person now is by following the ground scent, i.e., tracking.

You can now extend the length of track up to a mile or so in stages over the next few weeks/months using a line of canes 100 to 200 yards apart to indicate the line that the missing person has walked. You can also increase the time between the person walking away and the dog being put on his track up to half an hour. Then try experimenting with a track laid across the wind and watch the way the dog works. He should position himself between one and five yards downwind of the actual track line and will often weave left and right without actually crossing over the line of track.

As soon as you are confident in the dog's ability to guide you, dispense with all but the first bamboo cane. This cane will help you to show the dog the commencement of the track. You can also try tracking at night and experiment with different terrains. The enjoyment of both dog and handler will increase as confidence grows and will enable the dog to express a natural instinct in a way that is beneficial to the family. Once trained, you should have no difficulty in finding friends who will walk (or even run) away and hide for you and your dog.

I should emphasize that all tracks are laid in as near a straight line as possible as we are essentially teaching the dog a pursuit track which is not a good method of teaching the more demanding (for both dog and handler) competition tracking where several changes of track direction occur and the dog is tracking for articles laid on the track. Pursuit tracking, however, is easier to train, is just as enjoyable and does not require a very experienced handler or expert line handling techniques and dogs love it.

Competition exercises

Heel on lead

Training your dog to do competition heelwork on the lead should duplicate training it to walk off the lead, but a lot of people have difficulty obtaining a consistent off-lead performance because the action of the lead and not the command "heel" has been inadvertently trained as the main association. Consequently, when the lead is removed, the association of walking to heel is removed with it. It is essential therefore that, first of all, the correct type of lead and slip collar are used (see page ???) and that when the dog is being trained, the clip on the lead attaching it to the dogs collar is hanging underneath the dog's neck. The reason being that when we come to unclip the lead for heel free, the slip collar takes up this position, with the large rings hanging underneath quite naturally. If the lead is held so that the clip on the lead is either at the side of the dog's neck or worse still held above the dog's neck, when the lead is removed the dog instantly recognizes this because the rings on the collar take up their natural position. We are attempting to train the dog so that is the command "heel" and not the lead that keeps the dog close to the handlers left leg.

Method 1. This method employs the use of a reward rather than correction and for that reason, an ordinary leather collar or half check collar (martingale) and lead may be used. I will describe the training using a ball, but any form of reward may be used providing this is something special (see training and learning). Start by having the dog on your left and walking forward using the dog's name and the command "heel". If he doesn't immediately move to join you, tease him with the ball and repeat the command. Continue walking forward letting him see the ball, held close to your left side but too high for him to grab. At any point that his attention drifts away from you, turn to your right, drop the lead and throw the ball. On the first few occasions that you do this your dog may well miss the ball being thrown completely, but once he realizes that the ball is likely to be thrown his attention will improve to the point where he dare not take his eyes off you.

The lead is now only used to control jumping up or over enthusiasm. The training sequence of figure of eights, right, left and about-turns and fast and slow pace are put into the sequence as for method 1. The point is that the dog must never know when or if the ball is about to be thrown so he has to pay attention.

We now have to progress to moving the ball out of sight into our left coat pocket. To do this, first clench your fist around the ball to shield it from the dog's view, only letting him glimpse it if his attention starts to wander. The next stage is to put your hand with the ball in it into your left pocket. Again, if the dog's attention wanders, bring your hand out and throw the ball. Even though he can no longer see it he must always believe it is there when you give the command "heel" and put your left hand on, in or near your pocket. When the time comes to go into a competition, tease the dog with the ball and *pretend* to place it in your pocket, then go and work the dog. When you have completed your work, sneak the ball back into your pocket, do a few yards of heelwork and throw the ball as a reward. With careful training the dog should walk to heel watching your left hand for the slightest movement indicating that the ball is about to be removed and thrown. If the dog shows any tendency to work too wide you can either shorten the lead to restrict his movement away from you or move the reward into your right hand. If the dog tends to work too close, try holding the reward in your left hand which is now slightly wide of your left leg. Left turns can best be accomplished by moving your left hand slightly rearwards, making the dog step back as you turn. The command "heel" is only used to indicate the possibility of the ball being thrown.

If obedience competitions are contemplated then the handler must learn the precise footwork necessary for absolute precision in the competition dog. The best plan here is to cut out several paper "footprints" and ask any experienced competitor to place these on the ground to indicate right and left foot placement on the various turns. Then go away and practice without training the dog until you can execute turns correctly without even thinking about it. Then train your dog to maintain an exact position in relation to your precise position throughout these turns using the same techniques as for the figure of eight. Fast and slow pace are first trained in a straight line until satisfactory, and then turns may be introduced as above. No different commands are necessary when changing pace, although it is helpful if the command "heel" is used prior to turning to inform the dog of your intention to change direction.

Method 2. With the dog positioned sitting on your left and lead and collar on correctly, step off smartly leading with your left foot giving your dog's name and the command "heel", "close", etc. Only snap the lead tight if the dog does not immediately respond to your command to move. When the dog is walking in the desired position, praise gently. If the dog maintains the correct position and looks up at you for a couple of paces, suddenly bend down on one knee and really make a fuss of him. Do not attempt to make him sit at this stage-we only want him to associate the fuss with walking to heel in a specific way; not for sitting. If the dog attempts to move ahead, speak the dog's name and command "heel" and immediately snap the lead directionally opposite to the dog's movement. By holding the lead only in the right hand the danger is that any correction that may be applied tends to be in a direction across the handler's body, making the dog "crab", i.e., walk with its bottom stuck out and its head angled across its handler. If you must hold the lead in your right hand, then your left hand will need to be used for rear-ward correction.

The way the command is used is also important as it can affect the dog's desire to look at you whilst doing heelwork. The command must never be used as correction because if you glare at the dog, bellow heel in a very stern voice and

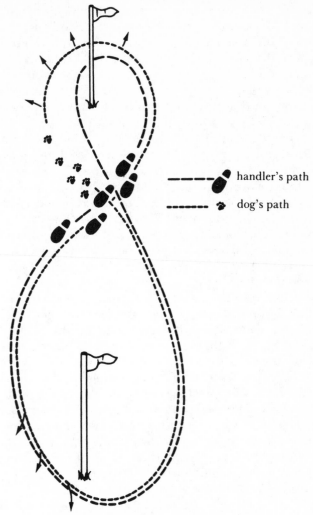

handler's path

dog's path

Figure 3 *Practise heel-on-lead turns round a figure-of-eight course*

then snap the lead tight, the dog will associate the unpleasantness with you and will start working with its head down instead of up. Ideally the command should be firm but pleasant. The lead suddenly snapping tight is the only disagreeable experience that the dog will try to avoid. As the dog continues to walk in a straight line, encourage him to concentrate on you by dropping your left hand and stroking the top of his nose and head at random intervals. For every few paces that the dog walks, giving 100 per cent concentration, stop and praise as above. As the dog's response starts to improve you can progressively reward for more and more steps with the dog watching you. It is always better to over reward at this stage rather than overcorrect.

Continue the training session for only a couple of minutes at a time until you progress to a hundred yards or so without having to correct and with the dog giving 100 per cent concentration. When you have achieved this, you can add to your dog's understanding of the command by incorporating right, left and about turns. The best way to start teaching the dog to maintain the correct position during these turns is by practicing around a figure-of-eight course. To do this, place two markers (bamboo canes) five yards apart and walk a figure-of-eight course, trying to describe two circles, one to the right, one to the left. During the right-hand part of the circuit you will need to use the lead to check the dog across your body as he will tend to drift wide. On the left-hand circle, check the dog as necessary by putting your left hand on the lead to slow him and stop him from leaning on your leg. Remember, try to encourage and reward, only using a command of heel to remind the dog of the position it needs to be in. Make sure that you stop and reward progress a little at a time. Once the dog has learned to maintain a consistent position during heelwork in a straight line or on a figure-of-eight course we can then start putting in 90-degree corners to left and right and the 180-degree about-turn both right and left.

Heel free

For the dog to adopt a position at heel when off the lead, the dog must be trained using the same associations as when on the lead. Our aim is to make the main association the command of "heel" and not the lead.

If you have used a compulsive method of training using a lead and collar as in method 2 then you will probably find it best to continue with this association when training heel free.

Method 1. Training a dog to do heel free using a system of reward is made much easier if a reward method has been used for heel on lead training. Try the following "game" of heel free. Hold a "reward" in your left hand.

Start with your dog at heel in the sit position. Walk forward giving your dog's name and a command. At any time that you feel that the dog starts to lose attention turn to your right and throw the reward down several yards in front of you. If you happen to be using food as a reward, you will need to place it in a small container so that the dog can easily see it as it lands. This will prevent the dog from having to sniff at the ground for his reward. Continue this training for a few minutes at each session until you can walk in a straight line at each of the three paces for a couple of hundred yards or so without the dog altering his position on your left. Remember that you do a right turn to throw the reward at any point that the dog even as much as looks away. You should, after several sessions, have the dog's undivided attention. Then try introducing right, left and about-turns, using the position of your left hand to control the position of the dog's head as in heel on lead (method 1). Be careful on right turns as the dog will tend to fly round expecting the reward to be thrown! For this to work successfully the dog must never be able to guess when (or if) the reward is about to be thrown, what it is going to be or how much he is going to get. He therefore has to watch all of the time in anticipation of this happening. The command "heel" tells him to move in to anticipate this reward.

Method 2. Start by placing your normal training lead and collar on the dog but in addition to this place a second, lighter collar and a fine nylon lead on as well. Tuck the nylon lead into your pocket and do a short training session of heel on lead. Then halt, place the dog into the sit position and remove the first lead and collar and put it in your pocket or around your shoulder. Then give your command and walk forward. If at any point your dog drifts wide or in front repeat the command and give the dog a really sharp jerk on the second lead. This experience conditions the dog into believing that he is still on the lead even though he has seen and felt the lead being removed. With some dogs, several leads may need to be put on and the dog checked each and every time he moves out of position "thinking" that he is no longer attached to you. The leads are taken off one at a time until eventually there is no lead attached at all, i.e., the dog is now doing heel free although mentally he is always on the lead when you give the command "heel". You then go through exactly the same sequence of training as for heel on lead with figure of eights, right, left and about-turns. The need for praise to encourage the dog to pay attention and look up at you whist working cannot be overemphasized.

Heelwork is as dull or exciting as you want to make it and the quickest way to bore the dog is by trudging up and down, turning right and left shouting the command "heel". We are, at these training sessions, only training the dog to walk to heel on command. Teaching the dog to sit on command or when you halt are trained at separate sessions. The quickest way to lose enthusiasm in heelwork is to put lots of halts and to praise the dog after each halt! In no way does that reward the dog for walking to heel; only for sitting.

The command sit

It might seem strange to explain various methods of training heelwork without mentioning the sit at heel, but it is quite easy to teach a dog to do heelwork and to sit when the handler halts without using a command at all. Look at it this way, if you want to work your dog at the top level of competition, you will have to train your dog eventually to sit at heel without a command. If you start by using a command, at some stage there will have to be a certain amount of retraining. Some people, therefore, prefer to train the dog to sit at heel without actually training the command "sit". So let us have a look at how we want the dog to interpret the command sit.

"Sit" should mean "Whatever you are doing, wherever you are, adopt a sitting position and remain in that position until I give you further instructions". "Heel" should then mean "Whilst I am walking, maintain a position alongside my left leg", "If I am stationary sit alongside my left leg".

So how can we teach the command sit?

Whichever method you use, you will need to start on the lead in order to minimize errors.

Method 1. Start with your dog on the left in the stand position. Give his name and the command "sit", and use your right hand to pull up on the lead and your left hand to push the dog's rear down onto the floor. His rear must be in a straight line with the direction you are facing, close to your left leg. It must also be on the floor within about a second of hearing the command. As soon as his bottom touches the floor praise gently, but do not let him lift it whilst you are praising him. He must learn not only to sit when told but to wait for a command before he moves. After a few seconds give him a command or signal to release him ("finish", "off you go", or a pat on the shoulder). Let him relax for a few seconds, position him at heel and repeat the command and action required.

With some dogs, a gentle slap on the rump is better than a push as there are dogs that brace themselves against the pressure of your hand. Repeat this several times at each training session until you reach a point where the dog starts to respond to, or even anticipate the command "sit". Now with the dog starting to obey the command, repeat the process with the dog standing in front of and facing you. Give the dog's name and command, pull up on the lead and lean forward to push or slap the dog into the sit position, trying to keep him facing and in line with you. Repeat at several sessions until the dog starts to associate the command with the action required. The thing to avoid at all costs is repeating the command more than once. If the dog does not respond to your first command, immediately show him what you want him to do. If you teach your dog to sit on the fourth or fifth command when the dog is on the lead and close by you, it will be virtually impossible to teach him to sit on command when he is fifty yards away from you.

The next step is to extend his knowledge of the sit command. With the dog at heel, command "sit" and take a pace to your right. If the dog shows any inclination to move out of the sit position and join you, lift the lead up high above the dog's neck and place the dog back into the sit, repeating the command. The trick is to check the dog as he first tries to move. If you have allowed him to get up and move towards you then make sure he receives a verbal warning and is put back into the same position that you left him in. If you are used to giving the universal command of "stay" then you may do so prior to walking away from your dog, although the stay command is not necessary.

Providing the dog eventually remains in the sit position where he was left, wait for a few seconds, then return to his side, wait for a further few seconds and then praise well making sure that the dog remains in the sit. If you allow him to stand up when you praise him he may well associate the praise with the act of standing and then start to stand on your return, anticipating the praise, instead of sitting, waiting for the praise. If the dog attempts to lie down then raise the dog back into the sit by using the lead, held high above his head.

Next try giving the sit command and then taking a pace in front of, and facing the dog. Repeat as above.

We can now start to extend his knowledge of the command further by walking him to heel on command, stopping and giving him his "sit" command, making sure that the dog's rear end is pushed in close to your left heel. To do this push or tap down on the outside of his flank in order to make his bottom move down and in towards you. When he is in the sit position it is important that he remains in that position until you either give him a further command of heel or a command or signal telling him that he is finished. With a little practice of a few minutes each day you should be able to get the dog to respond to the command sit whatever he is doing whilst on the lead. The next stage if you are obedience orientated is to teach the dog to sit from the down position. To do this, place the dog into the down (see page 129) on the lead. Wait a few seconds and then use the sit command and a few little tugs on the lead to get him to respond correctly. Always reward profusely whenever the dog makes any attempt to rise into the sit position. As this training progresses you can extend the time between the dog obeying the command and going forward to praise him.

Training the sit position is now extended in three different ways.

1. Extend the length of time and distance when leaving the dog in the sit position (sit stay) and start to provide distractions by getting other people and dogs to walk around. If the dog attempts to move then correct verbally, but not by shouting the command sit in a threatening tone. Never use the dog's name when you are away from him as this will usually confuse the dog with recall training. There is absolutely no point in removing the controlling influence of the lead until the dog is consistently remaining in the sit position for three minutes with you several feet away. The next stage is to leave the lead on, but trailing on the floor so that if the dog moves you are still in control within a few seconds. Leaving the lead on the floor also gets the dog used to obeying the command without seeing you holding the other end. When the dog obeys the sit command consistently for three minutes with you twenty paces away you can remove the lead. Remember that you must watch your dog like a hawk and be ready to verbally correct him if he tries to move by growling "Ah! No!" or "Bad dog" at him.

Praise well whenever you return, but keep him in the sit to do so. When you decide to teach the "sit stay out of sight" you should already have a dog that is very steady when left in sight. The first few sessions should involve you leaving the dog and standing beside a visual barrier for a few seconds. You then walk out of sight for only two seconds and then return and praise well or correct, depending on the dog's response to being left alone. Repeat several times until there is no movement by the dog. You can the extend the time you leave the dog each session by a few seconds. It is helpful to have a peephole so you can watch and if necessary correct the dog whilst he cannot see you. All of this training assumes that the dog has picked up the correct association at each stage of training. Some don't, in which case refer to "Stay problems", page 134.

*   *   *

2. Sit at a distance. With this training start with the dog wandering around the house or garden. Leave the lead and collar attached, but do not hold on to it. Whenever the dog's attention is not on you, sneak up within range of the lead, give the dog's name and the command sit, and at the same time pick up the lead. If the dog doesn't instantly respond then put him in the sit position, wait a few seconds then praise well. It is extremely important that when he hears his name and the command he is not allowed to move towards you but must remain where he was when the command sit was given.

Continue several times at each session and also include any time that the dog may be laying down naturally (not whilst asleep or resting).

As his response to the command improves you can increase the distance between you both but make sure that if the dog does not react quickly to the command or starts to come towards you, you go to the dog as quickly as possible without causing panic and show him the response required. When he responds to the command every time within about ten yards with the lead trailing you can the remove the lead. Slowly extend the distance up to anything you desire and then introduce minor distractions. Always praise well for the correct action. Always insist that the dog remains in the sit position until you go to him and praise. Never call him to you after telling him to sit at a distance.

3. Sit whilst walking to heel. Start by walking in a straight line for a distance of fifty yards. Every ten paces or so halt and give your command to sit, wait until the dog is in position and then walk in a circle around it once at the extremity of your lead. Praise well and continue a further four times. At each training session shorten the interval between giving your command and circling the dog until you can give the command without stopping or hesitating at all in the know-ledge that the dog will quickly sit and remain there until rewarded. You can then shorten the praise between the dog sitting and commanding heel to make the dog walk again. When the dog is responding correctly you can dispense with the lead and extend the diameter of your circle. The result

should be that when walking to heel the dog should obey your sit command whether you halt or continue walking in a straight line, about-turn, walk past him about-turn and collect the dog with a further "heel" command. When you get to this stage do not forget to occasionally finish and reward the dog without giving the "sit" command.

Method 2. The sequence of training is exactly the same as for method 1 only the technique of getting the dog into the sit position is different. This method involves the use of a reward, which may be either a toy or food. Start off by holding the reward above the dog's head, just out of reach and giving the dog's name and the command sit. Move slightly towards the dog raising the reward as you go until the dog adopts the sit position, then either give the food or throw the toy.

In a fairly short space of time the dog should learn to put his rear on the floor when the reward is produced, but may or may not associate the command sit with the action required. In other words it may be possible to hold the reward and say "rhubarb" and get the dog to respond by sitting, even if he has never heard the word rhubarb before. So the next stage is to put the reward into your pocket, give the dog's name and the command sit and put your hand into your pocket to produce the reward. You can then delay the production of the reward until the dog responds by sitting on the command "sit" anticipating that your hand will move into your pocket for the reward that he can no longer see. The best pocket to use especially for heelwork is the left-hand coat pocket, or trouser pocket for small breeds.

The down position

First of all a word of warning about the down position. As it is a position of submission, never attempt to train a dominant dog to adopt this position using force if the dog is already showing signs of aggression towards you until you have read Chapter 2, "Behaviour".

I will describe four methods of getting a dog to lie down

on command, three using guided learning, all using rewards. All four, initially start with dog in the sit position.

1. Place the thumb and forefinger of your left hand over and across the dog's shoulders, just behind his shoulder blades. Give the name and command, press down and sideways, rolling the dog down onto one flank. Wait a few seconds and reward him without letting him get up. He must associate the praise for staying down, never for getting up. Be sure to make sure your finger and thumb are positioned correctly; far forward and the dog will merely brace itself against the downward pressure, too far back and you will hurt him. A submissive dog will be the easiest of all to train the down on command. Repeat exactly as for the sit position from start to finish.

2. Place your left hand, palm down onto the dog's shoulders and your right hand on his chest close to his collar. Press down with the left hand and pull down with the lead. Repeat as above.

3. Kneel on the floor alongside your dog. Place your left hand palm down on the dog's shoulders. Pass your right hand behind the dog's front leg nearest to you and lightly grip the far front leg just above its paw. Move the right arm forward and press down with the left hand. This will "sweep" the dog's front legs forward, putting him into the down. Repeat as for 1.

4. Place your right hand with a tasty morsel in it, palm down on the floor in front of the dog. Gently place your left hand on the dog's shoulders. Encourage him by removing your right hand and showing him the food for a few seconds, then cover it up. When he puts his nose down to investigate, push gently with the left hand. As soon as the dog is down, lift your hand and let the dog eat the food. Repeat as for sit training, noting that whenever the dog is told to lie down at a distance from you it is important to go up and "find: a morsel of food on the ground between its front legs for him to eat, This method is only one that I would recommend for a very dominant dog as it avoids confrontation between dog and handler.

Figure 4 *Methods of teaching the down position*

The down training then continues in the same sequence as for the sit position.

The stand position

Once again we are going to look at the stand position trained during heelwork, at a distance and as a stay position and will review two different methods of achieving this.

Method 1. Start with the dog sitting at heel on the left with the lead on. Bend down and place the palm of your left

(a)

Figure 5a   *Teaching the stand position, method 1*

hand against the bend of stifle on your dog's closest hind leg. Hold the lead in your right hand close to the dog's collar. Press his hind leg backwards with your left hand, whilst preventing forward or sideways movement with your right hand. Praise gently as the dog rises into the stand position. Continue to praise gently for a few seconds before releasing him. If he attempts to sit, try not to correct him too harshly as he will become more and more unsteady. Progress slowly until he will stand on your command with only the lightest pressure on the front of his hind leg. Never put your hand over his back to touch the far hind leg as this will be too much like the association you have used to teach the sit position. Always keep the dog in the stand position for several seconds whilst quietly and gently offering praise.

Repeat as for the sit position, method 1, noting that when you come to teach the stand from the down position, you must also use the lead to encourage him to rise on his front legs first. When you progress to teaching the stand whilst walking to heel it helps if you use your left calf to touch the dog's stifle as the command is given so that the dog still associates the command with the action required.

Method 2. Obtain a two-inch-wide piece of webbing about six feet in length. With the dog in the stand position pass one end under his tummy, lifting it up on the far side to

A gun being fired can be a pleasant or unpleasant experience depending on the dog's association with it

Above and below: Right redirection. Some handlers use whistles, hand signals or voice commands or combinations of the three

Below and below right: Down stay trained using compulsion (Collie) and reward (GSD). The end result is the same but which dog looks happier?

A typical example of a chase instinct that the owner failed to control during early games of chasing a ball

Dogs do not learn by watching other dogs work but the excitement created can be used to increase a dog's motivation to work. The dog fastened up will do anything for a game with the other dog's toy

A GSD failing an 'intelligence' test. In order to reach the food bowl he must move away from it to unfasten the line from around the post. Dogs do not possess a 'thinking' mind and are incapable of solving such problems

(b)

Figure 5b   *Teaching the stand position, method 2*

form a sort of sling. Leave the lead attached to the dog's collar and held in the right hand. Hold both ends of the sling in your left hand. Give the dog's name and command and very gently give a few little tugs on the sling. The idea is not to lift the dog into the stand position, but almost to tickle him with the sling in order to made him stand. You can then use the lightest pressure to keep him standing as you follow the same sequence of training as for the sit. An advantage of this method in teaching the stand at a distance is that you can suspend your sling in a doorway, passing a light length of line through a hook in the top part of the frame. If you hold the other end of the line in your hand you can give the stand command at a distance and use the line to put a slight amount of pressure on the sling to get the dog to rise into the stand from either the sit or down positions. Always remember to reward well when you obtain the correct response, and be very gentle on applying any correction as this will tend to induce the dog to either sit or go down.

Stay problems

We can deal with these problems under two headings.

1. Dogs that get up and go towards their handlers
2. Dogs that remain where they are but break the positions they were left in.

Dealing with the first problem we need to understand why the dog wants to get to its handler. It could be either insecure in being left, possibly with other "strange" dogs or people, or it may well just simply want the reward that the handler has in his pocket that has been used to train the recall.

If the dog is nervous then you will need to remedy this before teaching the stay exercise. Clearly the best way of curing the problem is to remove the reward from the handler's pocket and put it in the dog's position. Look at it this way, if your dog moves during the exercise and you take the dog back to the place it dislikes and punish it, would you expect it to want to stay there? Of course not. That particular spot becomes even more unpleasant to the dog because its gets shouted at when it is there. The problem is worse if the handler has a reward in his pocket. The only place the dog wants to be is where the handler and reward is; the last place he wants to be is that nasty area between two dogs with other people around. So what we can do is to put the reward (food, ball, etc.) immediately in front of the dog and teach him not to touch it until you return to him.

The dog will now begin to prefer the place he is left to the place his handler is and will wait quite patiently for the handler's return to be given his reward.

How about the dog that does not actually come out of the stay to join his handler but simply alters its position? For a dog that lies down from the sit or stand position you could teach food refusal! Teach the dog not to touch food placed on the ground until you give it to him. You can start with his food at mealtimes. Then leave him in a sit or stand stay with a small container of food placed between his front paws. Growl "No" or something similar if he attempts to touch the food. He cannot lie down as he must avoid the food; he should not edge forward as his reward is in front of him. Return and feed him. Next progress to a small piece of liver placed on the ground, and finally to only the smell of liver from your finger and thumb rubbed on the ground. Every time (except in competition) you return, have a small piece of liver in your hand and pretend to pick it up from between the dog's front legs and feed him. This also works like a dream for a dog that edges forward in any of the stays. For a dog that rises from the down or sit, particularly when you go out of sight, try leaving the dog, going out of sight and sneaking around, out of the dog's vision in order to end up out of sight a few yards behind it. The dog will be concentrating on where you went out of sight and if it breaks position you can give a second command thereby giving the dog a mild shock. You can alternatively get a second person to act as a steward and place the dog back into position if it breaks.

If your dog breaks any stay to fight or sniff other dogs, etc., this is a behaviour problem (see Chapter 2)

If you have trained each of the sit, down and stand positions correctly as individual exercises you can now start to link the exercises together whilst walking to heel (advanced stand, sit and down); at a distance (distance control); at the end of a sendaway to control the position the dog in the down for obedience or in any position for trials; for stays either in or out of sight; for the present on recall or retrieve; for positions at the far side of jumps; to position the dog for speak on command and steadiness to gun.

Novice recall (Recall to front)

Assuming that your dog has been trained to remain in the sit or down position and is reasonably steady and has been trained to understand and obey the sit command whilst in front of and facing you, recall training can commence. We will break the exercise down into three parts: 1. stay, 2. recall to front, 3. finish to heel.

Method 1. Leave the dog in either the sit or down position and halt and about-turn ten paces or so away to face the dog. Have a tasty tidbit in your hands, which are held low in front of you. Place your feet about twelve inches apart. Give your dog's name and a command of "come", "here", "in", etc.

Bend your knees and hold out your arms to show the dog the food. As he comes toward you, draw your hands in to you and raise the food so that it is just too high for the dog to reach. At the same time straighten your knees and command "sit".

As soon as he is in the sit position give him the food. Do not be tempted to touch him if he tries to go past you but simply about-turn, take a pace backwards and try again. Do not bend over the dog as this will ultimately cause him to sit too far away from you.

Repeat several times until you are satisfied that the dog is starting to understand what is required.

The chances are that within a short space of time the dog will start to anticipate being called for the reward and will break the stay position. In order to minimize this causing a problem during "stays". you can start standing sideways on to the dog during stays, only facing the dog on a recall. Most dogs will then soon learn to make the distinction between when they are going to be called and when they have to stay just by watching which body position the handler adopts.

The finish to heel is trained as a separate exercise. To achieve this, start by getting your dog to sit at heel and then stand immediately in front of him. Hold some food in both hands and hold both hands in front of your body. Give the dogs' name and command heel and move your right hand around behind your back, encouraging the dog to follow it around. Transfer the dogs attention to your left hand behind your back and continue encouraging the dog around until he is in the heel position. Then raise your left hand and command sit. When the dog's bottom is on the floor give him the food. Repeat several times at each session. As the dog's response to the command improves you can omit the food in your right hand, but continue to move that hand to maintain the association with the response required from the dog. If your dog starts to come round too far and ends up almost sitting in front of you again, guide his bottom to the floor as he is in the correct position. Dogs only make mistakes if you allow them to.

Method 2. Leave the dog in the sit or down position, but attach a five-yard length of thin cord to his collar. Turn and face the dog, placing your foot on the end of the line. As you give the command "come". bend down pick up the line and give a gentle tug. As soon as the dog is moving towards you, praise and encourage him. If he stops, or tries to go past you, repeat the tug on the line. As he gets close to you it is easy to use the line to steer the dog into the correct position, but try to use more praise and encouragement than force. The finish to heel is trained as a separate exercise.

Start by putting the dog on a lead and get him to sit at heel. Then stand immediately in front of him. Hold the lead in your right hand, give the command heel and take a pace backwards with your right leg. At the same time give a gentle tug on the lead to start the dog moving in the required direction. Once the dog's head is level with your right leg, transfer the lead to your left hand behind your back and move your right foot back to its original position. Give a gentle tug on the lead with your left hand to help the dog move around the back of your legs. As the dog comes around into the heel position, change the lead back into your right hand and use your left hand to position the dog's bottom as you give the sit command. Praise well and repeat several times at each session. As the dog's response improves you can reduce and finally eliminate the movement of your right foot and also use the lead less and less each time until you can remove it altogether.

Whichever method you decide to use it is important that the three exercises (stay, recall, finish to heel) are not linked together until the dog has learned each one separately.

Recall problems

We can divide all recall problems into each of the three exercises.

1. Stay

a) Dog breaks stay position in anticipation of being called.
Cure

Dispense with recalls for a few sessions and work on the stay position. Use body posture to indicate whether stay or recall is required (see end of method 1). Vary time between positioning yourself for recall and calling the dog. If the dog anticipates on the steward's or instructor's command of "call your dog", get someone to keep repeating these words in training and call the dog after your "steward" has repeated the words several times.

b) Dog refuses to move on your command and remains in the position he was left.
Cure

Leave a collar and lead attached and, when you call the dog, get someone to act as a steward and give the dog a gentle tug to start him on his way. Praise well as soon as he heads towards you.

2. Recall

a) Dog comes in very slowly.
Cure

Use more reward, less compulsion, particularly on the straight sit in front.

b) Dog charges in too fast.
Cure

As the dog approaches, take a quick step forward in to the dog. After several repetitions the dog will still come in quite fast, but slow down as he approaches anticipating your step forward.

c) Dog sits crooked in front.
Cure

If the dog always sits crooked to one side, to your right for instance, place your right foot forward with the toe pointed upwards to prevent your dog sitting crooked to that side. It is useless to let the dog sit crooked and then try to straighten him up. Prevention is better than cure. If the dog often sits crooked but favours no particular side, try placing two short bamboo canes in the ground eighteen inches apart and a yard in front of you. It now becomes impossible for the dog to learn to sit crooked.

3. **Finish to heel**

a) Dog anticipates finish to heel.
Cure
Keep the dog sitting in front for any random length of time up to a minute before sending him to heel. Occasionally,finish the exercise with the dog sitting in front without sending him to heel.

b) Dog goes wide to heel.
Cure
Put the lead on to check any wide movement, or stand close to a wall to prevent the dog moving wide.

Retrieve

To be successful when training a dog to retrieve it is essential that a good, free-running recall is achieved first. The novice recall only forms a very small part of retrieve association and there must be many trainers whose dogs do an excellent recall to front under controlled conditions but whose dogs will not return correctly with a dumbbell. The reason is that most dogs at the start of training view running to chase a thrown article as a game. If we cannot control a dog that is running free and playing we are going to find it difficult to obtain a good controlled retrieve.

To get a good retrieve we can use a play or reward method as in the retrieve under the pet-training section, but modifying it as follows.

Method 1. When the dog is at the stage where it is retrieving reasonably well, place a light nylon lead on him before throwing the article and then let him run out with the lead attached. When he returns, pick up the lead and take a few steps backwards until he is close to you and perfectly straight. Give a command of sit, using the lead under the dog's chin to support his lower jaw and assist him into the desired position. Really praise him well if he maintains his grip on the dumbbell/article. Continue praising for a few seconds before taking the article. He must associate the praise with holding and not releasing. If he drops the article before you take it or when you make him sit, pick it up and gently put it back into his mouth and praise well before taking it.

Method 2. If you have a dog that has no natural retrieving desires or who is easily distracted by its surroundings, or by people and other dogs, you will have to use the trained retrieve. This method enables any dog to be trained to retrieve provided there are no underlying behaviour problems or physical problems with the dog's mouth (teething etc.). If you have a dog that is showing signs of dominance towards its owners, this must be corrected before retrieve training can commence (see Chapter 2 "Behaviour").

Obtain a piece of broom shank or dowel or rolled-up carpet about six inches long. Place the dog in the sit position on your left and attach a lead to its collar. Put your left arm over the dog's shoulders and bring your left hand under the dog's bottom jaw. Press the dog's jowls with your thumb and second finger just behind the canine teeth. The dog's mouth should open just enough for you to push thumb and finger into the dog's mouth, rolling his jowls over his teeth. He cannot bite your fingers now as he will bite himself first. Gently praise him all the while. Once he has accepted your finger and thumb opening his mouth after a couple of sessions, pick up the retrieve article and gently pop it into his open mouth letting it rest behind his canine teeth. Support his lower jaw with your left hand and stroke the top of his head and nose with your right hand. Praise and reassure him all the time he is holding it correctly. If he tries to spit it out or chew it, immediately stop stroking him and growl

"Bah" at him in a very stern voice. Do not let the article come out of his mouth. When he is holding properly praise gently, wait for a few seconds and take it from him. Never praise after removing the article, all the praise must be for holding it. Try to use the tone of your voice for praise and correction and do not try and clamp the dog's jaws together as this will immediately make him want to fight against the article in his mouth.

After a few sessions he should get the idea that holding the article is preferable to trying to chew it or spit it out. You can then start to use a command of "hold" or "fetch" each time you place it in his mouth. Remember, if he tries to spit it out you must not bellow "hold" at him; we do not want him to associate the command hold with punishment. Always give the command "hold" in a pleasant tone. If your timing is split-second he should realize that when you say hold he must open his mouth to take the article. If he holds it gently and maintains his grip on it he should feel that he is the best dog that has ever been born because of your praise. If he tries to drop it or chew it he should instantly feel that all rewards instantly stop. All this is achieved by using the tones and words "Good boy", "Clever dog" etc. or "Bah".

The purpose of the right hand stroking the dog's nose and head is to make the dog want to look up. It is when his head falls that he is most likely to drop the article.

As you progress, try lowering your left hand from under the dog's jaws and stroking his side with it. Then when the dog is able to hold the article for thirty seconds or so without any problems, combine the hold with a short sit stay on the lead. If your dog discovers that it can avoid having the article placed in its mouth by reversing away from you, train the dog up against a wall. Once the dog has mastered the sit and hold with you several yards away, we can progress to the next stage.

Leave a lead on the dog, place the article in his mouth with a command of hold, walk away to the end of the lead and then turn and face him. Give your recall command and gently pull the lead and encourage the dog to move towards you. Use the lead under his lower jaw to keep his head up and to prevent him releasing his hold on the article. When

he is close in front of you give him a sit command, praise
well then take the article from him. If your dog drops the
article as he starts moving towards you, quickly alter the tone
of your voice, replace the article in his mouth and repeat.
Remember only to use your voice to correct or praise. It is
possible that if you growl at the dog for dropping the article
he will associate your correction with moving towards you
and not with dropping the article at all. So it is more than
possible that when you replace the article in his mouth he
will not drop it but neither will he move towards you. Coax
and encourage as much as possible only using the lead if
necessary. If the dog drops the article when you get him to
sit in front, try extending your right hand under the dog's
lower jaw as he comes towards you and gently lift his head
as you give the sit command. When, after several sessions,
you have a steady recall and hold you can progress to teaching the dog to run out to pick up and retrieve a thrown
article.

You must now substitute your article for a proper dumbbell. If you examine a dumbell you will notice that when it
is thrown, it lands on the ends with the centre portions
raised above the ground. This enables the dog to pick up
the dumbbell easily without having to "scrape" it up from
the floor.

With the dog on the lead, place the dumbbell on the
ground a yard or so in front of you. Give the dog's name
and the hold command and take the dog forward using your
left hand to gently encourage him to put his head down
towards the centre bar on the dumbbell. As the dog's mouth
touches the dumbbell use the thumb and forefinger of your
right hand to open the dog's mouth so that the dumbbell slides in. Give the dog lots of praise when he lifts the
dumbbell off the floor. Repeat several times until the dog
anticipates your hand coming down to open his mouth and
does so by himself. Then, as he picks the dumbbell up,
quickly run a few yards away and call him to you, getting
him to sit for praise before you take the bell from him. You
may well need to be quite patient in insisting that the dog
puts his head down to pick up the dumbbell, but the dog
will soon accept this providing that you really go overboard

with praise, when he is responding correctly. If he drops the dumbbell when he is moving towards you or when he sits in front, make *him* pick it up again.

As you progress at each session, make the dog move ahead of you to pick up the dumbbell by applying a forward and downward pressure on the lead. It is sometimes helpful if you get a friend to take the dog out to pick up the dumbbell each time you throw it to help build up the retrieve association in the dog's head. For the final stage, remove the lead, throw the dumbbell and, as soon as it lands, send the dog with your retrieve command, Take a pace forward if necessary put your finger through the ring on the dog's collar to propel him forward. As he picks up, praise well then use your recall command followed by the command sit as he returns. Praise well and wait for a few seconds before taking the dumbbell. Then use your finish to heel to position the dog for the next retrieve.

Retrieve problems

1. *Dog anticipates handler's command to retrieve*

Cure

Simply get someone to stand several yards away from you and give your controlling command. Throw the retrieve article, and each time the dog breaks his position have your helper pick up the article, thereby denying the dog the opportunity to retrieve it. After several sessions the dog should learn that moving before the retrieve command is given means that he can never get the article. In competition you will generally have a judge/steward standing somewhere near where the article is thrown, thus maintaining the association in the dog's mind.

2. *Dog is very slow in returning after picking up article*

Cure

Too much compulsion has been used to get a straight present. Forget about the dogs position in front and simply turn and run away as the dog picks the article up to recreate the dog's enthusiasm to return. The same technique should be adopted on the recall.

3. *Dog brings the article in but drops it in front as it sits*

Cure

Practice only the last yard of the dog's return with the dumbbell using the lead to maintain control. Leave the dog in the stand position with the article in its mouth, and back away only a yard. Call the dog, using the lead under his bottom jaw to prevent the dog releasing its grip. Command sit and ensure that you encourage the dog as it moves into this position. If the dog attempts to release its hold as it sits, growl "Bah" at it. Do not let it drop the article. Praise as soon as the dog is sitting. Leave the article in it's mouth and repeat the process several times.

4. *Dog picks the article up but will not return with it*

Cure

Forget the retrieve and practice the free-running recall.

5. *Dog pounces on the article, knocking it forward in the process*

Cure

Either put the dog on a length of fine line and give it a little check as it approaches the article in order to slow it down, or always throw the article so that it lands against a barrier (wall, fence, etc).

6. *Dog chews the article as it returns*

Cure

Re-teach the hold from the beginning. A dog only chews because the handler has over emphasized the enthusiasm or play aspect of the exercise.

Recall to heel

When training a dog to carry out this exercise, most people leave the dog in the sit position when they walk away. At the top level of competition the only recall to heel is carried out from the down position after sendaway, so it may be as well to train the dog to recall from this position right from the start.

Method 1. Start by having some form of reward in your left hand, Unclip the lead and leave the dog in your chosen position. After several paces give the dog's name and your heel command, without altering your stride and offering the reward if necessary to get him moving towards you. When the dog is within a couple of yards of your left leg, turn left and continue walking and encouraging him to remain in the heel position for several more yards then give him his reward.

The purpose of the left turn is to slow the dog's final approach and to prevent him running past your leg.

As his response improves you can delay the left turn until he has taken several paces in the correct position after he has joined you. When the dog has learned to move into the correct position without the necessity of the left turn you can start to teach the right turn.

Start by leaving the dog in your chosen position, walk away and after several yards call the dog to heel. As soon as he is in the correct position, turn right and reward after a few paces. After a few repetitions you can start turning right just before the dog reaches you, holding your left hand out if necessary to ensure that the dog moves around your body and does not cut across in front of you. Progress slowly until the dog always moves into the correct position, even if you turn right with the dog still several yards away from you. You can then extend the heelwork after the dog has joined you, and include left, right and about-turns before rewarding him.

Method 2. The sequence of training is the same as for method 1, but this time using a twelve foot length of cord.

Attach the line to the dog's collar and stretch it out on the ground in front of the dog. Leave him in your chosen position and walk away. Just as you reach the end of the line, give his name and your heel command and bend down to pick up the end of the line. Continue walking forward and give a tug on the line to start him moving towards you. If the dog tries to dash past you can again use the line to correct this. Continue sequence as for method 1. As the dog's response to the command improves you can shorten the line length or replace the line with a light nylon training lead and allow the lead to trail as the dog moves towards you on its recall. If the dog fails to take up the correct position at heel you can swiftly pick up the trailing lead and give a sharp reminder to the dog as you repeat the command.

Recall to heel problems

1. *Dog anticipates recall*

Cure

To prevent anticipation go through the training sequence of leaving the dog, turning left, right, about etc., without calling the dog to heel. Return and reward for staying. Only call the dog 50 per cent of the time in training, returning and rewarding the other 50 per cent.

2. *Dog is slow to join handler*

Cure

Use more reward, less correction. Try running away as you call the dog. As he approaches, throw a ball so that he dashes past your left leg after it. As soon as you have built up his enthusiasm then carefully introduce control as in the method above.

Sendaway (Obedience)

In common with most advanced exercises, the sendaway to a marked area is a combination of exercises comprising the following: 1) sendaway, 2) drop or down on command, and 3) recall to heel.

In order to start sendaway training it is important that the initial training presupposes the dog has already been trained to drop on command and recall to heel. If this is not the case then these exercises must be trained separately from the basic sendaway.

Method 1. Any form of reward may be used for this method, but I shall describe the process using food.

To start with, we must make the dog want to run away from its handler because its reward is somewhere inside a marked area. Unfortunately, this is where a lot of trainers fall down when using food because they make the exercise one of nosework instead of eyesight. I will describe my process from start to finish.

Start by marking out a "box" using white posts, pop bottles or housebricks, etc., spaced about four feet apart to form corners. Place a white sheet of paper, big enough to be clearly visible to the dog, in the centre of the box.

Take the dog up on the lead and drop a piece of food onto the paper and let the dog eat it. Praise it as it does so. Now place a second piece of food on the paper, but prevent the dog from touching it by restraining it on the lead. Walk backwards a few paces, sit the dog at heel, unclip the lead and give your chosen sendaway command. As the dog approaches the paper in the centre of the box praise well and join him as he is eating.

Continue for two or three sessions, slowly extending the distance that you send the dog up to about ten yards. Always go forward and praise the dog as he reaches the box.

Now hold the dog about ten yards away and get a helper to place the food on the paper before sending the dog. Extend the distance to thirty yards over a further two or three sessions.

The next stage is to place food underneath the paper before sending the dog. He will still run forward and reach the paper and will still possibly be able to smell the reward, only this time he will need your help to obtain it. Run up and lift the paper to let him get the food. Praise well and repeat for several sessions.

The next stage is to repeat the sendaway without any food underneath the paper. As the dog reaches the centre of the box, run forward with a reward concealed in your hand, lift the paper and pretend the food has come from underneath.

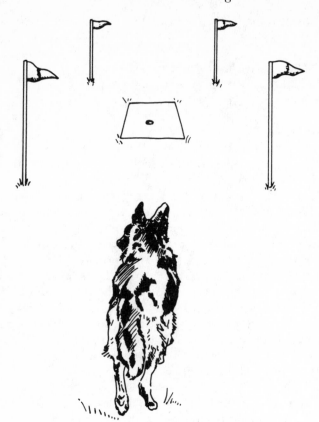

Figure 6 *Teaching the sendaway using a 'box'
and white paper*

So after a few further sessions we have eliminated the smell of food from the paper completely, but the dog still expects you to find his reward under it and is happily running forward in anticipation of you joining him to help him locate it.

Over the next few sessions, reduce the size of the paper. Now that the main association is being reduced the markers on the corners of the box will be used by the dog to locate the reward, i.e. he should have learnt that the reward is always contained within the marked area. When you finally remove the paper in the centre of the box you must start to introduce the drop on command. Sit the dog alongside your left leg facing the sendaway. Give him his command, and when he reaches the centre of the box give him the down command. As soon as he drops, run up with food concealed in one hand and pretend to find it on the ground between the dog's front legs.

Repeat using as many different corner markers as possible. If ever the dog misses the sendaway box, make him lie down where he is, walk to the centre of the box and pretend to find the food in the centre, calling the dog to you as you do so. Do not let him actually touch the food, but tease him with it and repeat the exercise only rewarding if the dog executes the sendaway to your satisfaction.

Method 2. This is a more compulsive method of training than method 1 and it involves teaching the dog to move away from you and lie down in a "safe" area indicated by four corner markers. Training the dog to drop on command separately is not necessary using this method, as it can be accomplished during all stages of training. You can start off in the house by having a small piece of carpet or mat about a yard square placed on the floor, preferably in a corner of the room. Get the dog used to lying on this piece of carpet at various times during the day and evening.

You can slowly progress, using a lead and collar. Take the dog and make it lie down on the carpet each and every time you give a sendaway command. After a few sessions, let go of the lead and point the dog at the carpet, from several yards away, then give the sendaway command. If the dog runs away from you and lays on the carpet, run up and really praise well. If he doesn't move or stops midway between you and the carpet, quickly pick up the end of the lead and use it to insist that he moves away in front of you until he reaches the carpet. Make him lie down and then praise well. As soon as the dog will move the length of the room to lie down on the carpet on your command, alter the position of the carpet within the room to remove any association of its location from the dog's mind.

As soon as you are satisfied that the dog understands that he is supposed to move away and lie on the carpet on your command then you can take dog and carpet to an outside location, marking the position of the carpet with four send-away markers placed to form a "box" at the extremity of the field/hall you are working in and not in the centre. Using the same techniques as for the initial training, start with the dog quite close to the box to begin with. Send the dog forward on command, and praise well if he enters the box and drops on the carpet as you give a "down" command. If he stops short, quickly run up and take him into the box, praising well as he goes down on the carpet. Continue the training until you can achieve a distance of about thirty yards. At each subsequent session cut the carpet down a few inches, until the dog eventually uses the corner marker, which up to now have only been of secondary importance, as the primary association with the sendaway has been the carpet. It is then important that you use several different sets of corner markers for training, and then train in as many different locations as possible both inside and out.

Sendaway problems (Obedience)

1. *Dog drops short of the "box"*

Cure

Mark several boxes one beyond the next and put the reward (method 1) just beyond the last set of markers, teaching the dog to pass through several sets of markers to reach his reward. If using method 2, place a square of carpet beyond the marked box and teach the dog to run straight through the box to get to the carpet.

2. *Dog stops short of the box*

Cure

Increase the reward (method 1) or increase the compulsion (method 2). If the problem is persistent change the method.

3. *Dog deviates from a straight line between handler and sendaway box*

Cure

Make the box more visual to the dog during the next few training sessions. Use the mechanical barrier, such as black thread stretched between the front markers and the handler's position to form a corridor out of which the dog may not deviate, even though he may not see the corridor visually.

4. *Dog enters box but turns out of the side to drop*

Cure

Use less compulsion on the down and more reward. If the dog associates the box itself with compulsion or punishment he will avoid it purposely. Change to method 1.

Scent discrimination

Out of all the obedience exercises, I feel that this is generally the least understood. It can be, and usually is, trained as a compulsion exercise following on from retrieve. A typical training session involves sending the dog to find and retrieve an article bearing a given scent. If the dog selects the wrong article, it is corrected, usually verbally. If it selects the correct article it is praised. It is hardly surprising therefore that many dogs fail to learn to make the correct decision themselves because the handler is making the decision for them in training. Look at it this way. If the dog picks up the wrong article and I shout at him and take it from him only to send him back to make a further selection, when he eventually brings the correct article, has he learnt to make that decision himself? I doubt it. He may simply have learnt to keep retrieving articles until I praise him. He may have learnt to glance at me before or after making "his" selection to check my facial expression to see if I approve. He may pick up the correct article and freeze, being unable to rely on his own ability in case he is wrong. There is also about a one-in-twenty chance that he will associate the particular smell of the article as being linked to a reward. What you must remember is that at each training session the dog will have learned something, but this probably will not be what we have wanted him to learn.

I will now describe a system of training which relies solely on reward during the decision-making process of the exercise.

You can use virtually any set of articles for scent training, but I will describe the process using cloths.

Start by rubbing a cloth lightly between the palms of your hands. Place it on the floor in front of the dog, place a small piece of liver on top of the cloth and then send the dog forward to eat the liver. It does not retrieve the cloth at this stage – the retrieve is trained separately. Repeat a few times and then place several more scented cloths and one "clean" (unscented) cloth in a line with the small piece of liver on all of the scented ones. Send the dog but say nothing until he has located the correct cloths and eaten the liver, then praise gently. Do not ask him to retrieve the cloths. At the next session place the cloths out, but put the liver underneath all of the correct cloths. The dog can spend as much time sniffing each cloth as he likes, but will immediately recognize the correct cloths because of the liver (primary association) and your scent (secondary association). As the dog starts to nose and paw at any of the correct cloths go forward and help him to get the reward from under it. Place up to ten scented cloths out with the unscented cloth placed at random anywhere along the line, and repeat several times. The dog should eagerly go forward and sniff each cloth carefully before making his decision, which of course will almost always be correct. In the extremely unlikely event of the dog becoming interested in a clean cloth, go up and lift the cloth to show the dog that there is no reward there. Continue until the dog is confidently finding the correct cloths and disregarding the clean one. He has a nine in ten chance of getting it right and so his confidence will increase.

The next stage is to place the cloths out without any liver underneath the correct ones, but have a small piece of liver concealed in your hand before you send the dog. He will go forward and smell each cloth in the manner that you have trained him to do, and when he reaches any correct cloth and starts to nudge it simply go up and pretend (by sleight of hand) that you have found the liver underneath the cloth.

After a few repetitions he should eagerly want to find the correct cloth every time, even though the smell of liver (now the secondary association) is completely absent and your scent (now the primary association) is all that the dog can smell. If, as is most likely, the dog selects the wrong cloth, show him there is not reward underneath.

The final stage is to send the dog with your chosen command, wait until the dog is nudging the correct cloth and then use your retrieve command to get him to bring it back to you. Forget about the sit in front, but simply take the cloth and pretend to "find" the liver inside it, right in front of his nose. A few more repetitions and he will soon be wanting to go out, find and return with the correct cloth every time. Again, if he makes an unlikely error, show him that there is no reward inside.

You can now reduce the number of correct cloths until there is only one correct one amongst the other clean cloths. You can also put in as many decoy (scented by another person) scent cloths as you wish even at the commencement of training, as the dog learns only to want the reward associated with your scent.

When it comes to giving your scent to the dog I fail to see why some people find it necessary to put their hand over the dog's nose. If your dog has no idea what you smell like stood alongside you, then there is never any hope of training him to use his nose in any exercise!

How about when we come to "C" scent where the dog has to take scent from one cloth and find and retrieve a similar one? Simple, just place the scented cloth on the floor and take the dog up and encourage him to smell it, then pretend to find liver underneath it as you lift it up. With the dog sufficiently excited, do a quick about-turn, pretending to throw the cloth if you wish and then send him. When the correct cloth is returned, you find the liver inside for him.

It is important that when the dog takes scent from the first cloth, he is not allowed to make contact with that cloth.

The practice of placing cloth over the dog's nose and even pumping his stomach to make him inhale is usually carried out by people who understand next to nothing about how good a dog's nose really is! If I put a petrol-soaked rag across your nose and made you breathe deeply several times, could you then go and distinguish between two or three different brands of after-shave? Of course you couldn't, at least not until you had blown your nose to rid it of excess scent or sneezed. Watch the number of dogs in Test "C" obedience competitions that have to do just that.

Long sendaway (Working Trials)

The most successful sendaway is accomplished by using a system of reward, but a lot of people fall down here by failing to obtain visual association with the reward. What happens then, is that the dog starts to use his nose instead of his eyes and the exercise quickly degenerates to one of nosework with the dog soon losing both distance and direction.

There is a compulsion method of training as in obedience sendaway method 2, but if this is to be embarked on it is important that some form of visual marker (single white post, road traffic cone, etc.) is used to indicate where the carpet is located. The problem of using compulsion is that because of the distance that the dog is required to move away from its handler, the dog can very easily avoid the compulsion, unlike the obedience equivalent where the dog remains quite close to its handler.

I shall therefore explain the reward system of training only.

To start with you only need a visual marker, a length of broomshank, painted white with one end sharpened to a point or alternatively with a six-inch nail hammered into the end with the head cut off (drill a suitable hole, slightly undersize into the broomshank first). This will enable the post to be stuck into the ground so that it stands upright. Now screw a few small, plastic-coated hooks into the post, about a foot apart. Next, obtain a soup ladle, plastic if possible, from a kitchen tool set. Take this training equipment

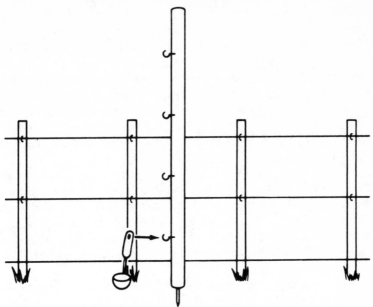

Figure 7   *Teaching the long sendaway using a*
broom handle and ladle

out with you and include some form of reward such as food
or a ball.

Push the sendaway post firmly into the ground close to
any natural boundary in the field you are in. Place the ladle
on the lowest hook and place the reward on the ladle. Position the dog a few feet from the post, point to the post and
send the dog forward to get his reward. Do not use a control
command when he gets there but simply run forward to join
and praise him whilst he is eating/playing with the ball. It
is important that he rewards himself and so the ladle must
be low enough to permit this at first.

Extend the distance in stages up to about one hundred
yards. It is vital in these initial training sessions that the post
is clearly visible and that the dog can reward itself when it
gets to the post. It is also extremely important that you always
go up to the post and praise the dog there, never call him
back to you to praise him.

Once you are satisfied that the dog is going the entire

distance on one command, without stopping, you can start raising the ladle higher up the post, removing the lower cup hooks as you go to prevent the dog catching himself on them.

Although the dog knows that his reward is attached to the sendaway post it is becoming increasingly difficult for him to reach it by himself and he will therefore start to become more dependent on his handler joining him to get the reward for him. With a large, athletic dog you may need to get a longer post!

After a few sessions we should reach a point where the dog will race to the post on command and wait there anticipating that his owner will eventually join him to give him the reward he can no longer get by himself. The next stage is to vary the location of the post within the field so that the dog doesn't build too great an association with that particular location.

We can then place the post with the reward in the field, out of sight of the dog. At the start of the session, bring him into the field and do perhaps a retrieve, heelwork, recalls, etc. Then position the dog for a sendaway, and point him at the post until he spots it. If he does so, then give him the sendaway command and release him. If he doesn't appear to have seen the post, go closer and try again until he does see it. Run up, praise and reward well after he has reached the post.

Extend the training into different locations, but always maintain the primary visual association with the post to encourage a fast, enthusiastic sendaway.

We now have to eliminate the post, but maintain the response to the command. There are two ways of achieving this. You can either find a field that rises towards the centre and then falls away on the far side so that the dog's view of the far fence is totally obscured by the natural contour of the land, or alternatively, you can use a field with gaps in the boundary hedge, leading into an adjoining field.

Position the sendaway post either at the far fence or beyond the gap in the hedge depending on the field. Now take the dog and position him so that from where you send him he cannot see the post at all, but the position must be carefully worked out in advance so that as soon as the dog has moved forward by about twenty yards the pole becomes visible. Set the dog up, pointing him in the desired direction and send him on command. Remember that he doesn't have to travel far in approximately the correct direction before the post suddenly comes into view. Move forward as the dog goes out to keep him in full view. Go forward to give him a reward from the post. Slowly increase the distance that the dog has to cover before seeing the post until the dog will happily move in excess of 150 yards before seeing the post and running to it. Don't forget that you are hopefully building in an association with the boundary fence, hedge, etc. of each field that you train in. If the dog has never found the post in the centre of the field, he will always assume that it is at it's extremity.

When you are confident that you can enter a strange field, set up the post so that it is not visible to the dog until he is twenty yards or so from it, bring the dog into the field and send him towards the post with reasonable accuracy and on one command, you may then wish to lose the association with the post completely. To do this simply remove the ladle from the post and tie a fairly long length of string through the hole in the top. You can now fasten the ladle to fence posts, telegraph posts, hedges, trees, etc., at the height the dog has been accustomed to. There is no chance of the dog seeing the ladle with its reward until it gets quite close, and so you can now condition the dog to run in the direction that you indicate to him until he reaches the boundary where his reward is waiting.

Remember that sendaway is not an exercise for a lazy trainer, you only get out of the dog what you put in. Keep sessions short and maintain the dog's interest. Train the control position (sit, stand or down) separately and only link the two exercises together when the dog understands each one perfectly. The recall is also trained separately and rarely, if ever, practiced as part of the sendaway sessions.

Sendaway problems

1. *Dog is poor at marking the sendaway point when set up for the exercise*

Cure

Make the sendaway point more visual.

2. *Dog stops on the way out and requires a second command to move*

Cure

Make progress in slower stages. You should not set out to test the dog during training sessions. Go back to shorter, happier sendaways for a while.

3. *Dog is not under sufficient control at the end of sendaway*

Cure

Train control at a distance but not as part of sendaway training, see Sit, and Down positions.

4. *Dog deviates from straight line or curves off and misses sendaway point*

Cure

If this happens whilst you are using a white post then you will need to make it even more visual. Try pinning a white carrier bag to the top. If the problem occurs when you have reduced or eliminated the post, try returning to the visual marker for a while and slowly alter the marker to a fence post, telegraph pole, etc.

5. *Dog does not run out willingly or refuses to move at all when sent*

Cure

Change the reward from food to a ball or vice versa. Make the dog **want to go**.

Redirection (Directional Control)

In order to reduce any possible confusion in the dog's mind it is important that redirection training is left until you are entirely satisfied with the dog's sendaway in terms of both distance and direction.

Redirection is trained as a separate exercise from sendaway with the two being linked only when the dog's response to sendaway, left and right direction commands is instant and correct.

Start by placing the sendaway pole up against a clearly defined boundary fence. Position the dog twenty-five yards or so away from the post but up against the boundary. It is immaterial which direction you train first, but assuming that it is going to be left the dog is positioned to the right of the post as above.

Stand a yard or two away from the dog and give your left command (usually accompanied by a signal with the left hand). As the dog moves to the post give some verbal encouragement, then go and help the dog recover the reward. Slowly and progressively move further back from where the dog is being positioned until the dog happily redirects twenty-five yards left with you 100 yards away. You can then progressively move the post further away from the dog's position at each session until he will cover 75 to 100 yards on your command. Always go to the post when the dog reaches it and reward well. Then go back to the beginning and teach the right redirect.

The next stage is to position the dog midway between two white posts, fifty yards apart against a boundary, one of which has a reward. Move back fifty yards or so and direct the dog to the post with the reward. If he moves in the correct direction praise and encourage the dog. If he makes a mistake, say nothing but wait until he gets there, go up to join him and show him there is no reward available. Reposition him in the centre and try again. Remember that the dog wants to move in the right direction to receive his reward. You should end up, after a few sessions, with the dog eagerly awaiting your command and signal telling him which pole the reward

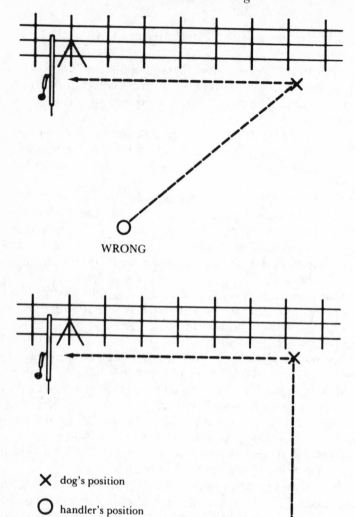

WRONG

X dog's position

O handler's position

RIGHT

Figure 8 *Teaching the dog to change direction at a distance*

is on and should soon get it right every time. The danger of shouting abuse at the dog if he makes a mistake in direction is that the dog may well refuse to try again because of the fear of moving incorrectly.

The next step is to go through a process of losing the association with the posts as for sendaway training.

Speak (Bark) on command

This is a simple exercise to train, particularly if you have a dog that tends to be a bit noisy when he gets excited such as when people come to the door, or when the lead is produced for a walk.

First fasten the dog on a collar and lead, tying the end of the lead around a fence post or any convenient point. Stand immediately in front of and facing him. Tease him with a favourite toy or food and then start walking slowly backwards calling him by name and trying to excite him with the reward.

As soon as he makes any noise at all even a whimper, quickly return and give the reward. Continue for a few sessions and then progressively alter the production of the reward so that he only gets it for barking and not for whining. At first a single bark will do, at which point you can introduce your command of "speak" as you back away. When you have achieved a reasonable level of consistency you can reward for every second bark, then every third bark until the dog barks continually on your command. You can then add variety to your training by progressing to off the lead in various positions, out of sight, walking to heel and so on.

Search

Let us first have a look at the requirements of the exercise. The dog is required to go into a marked area to locate and retrieve a number of small articles handled by, as near as possible, a stranger to the dog. A good enthusiastic retrieve is a pre-requisite of the exercise on all the articles the dog is likely to be asked to find in the search square. There is

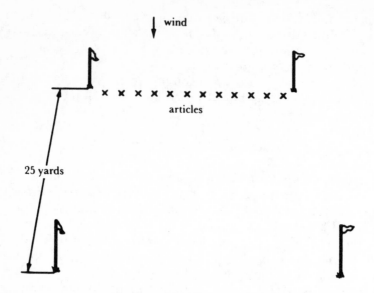

Figure 9   *Teaching the dog to search*

no point in placing a spark plug in the square for the dog to find unless it has been trained, quite separately, to retrieve it.

Start by throwing a reasonable-sized article into fairly lush grass and facing into the wind. Let the dog watch the article land send him in to find and retrieve it. Repeat this several times, teasing the dog with the article before throwing it each time. The next stage is to throw the article, but delay sending the dog for several seconds in order to start eliminating the visual "marking" process. Progress by doing a couple of about turns on the spot, between throwing the article and sending the dog, to disorientate him. He will remember roughly where the article has landed, but will now have to use his nose to locate it. As soon as the dog is reasonably proficient you can add a second similar article. Face the dog into the wind and throw each article in turn so that they land a couple of yards apart.

Turn the dog around once or twice before sending him in to find and retrieve the first article. Praise well when he brings it out, send him round to heel and whilst he is round the back of you, pretend to throw the article back into the area. Send the dog once more, encouraging him only when necessary, until he locates and retrieves the second article. You can now start to increase the number of articles in the area up to about ten.

There is no need for the dog to recover all of the ten articles as long as he is praised as soon as he recovers each article and has worked for a few minutes. You can finish the session with the dog still willing to find more. You will now need four search poles and the services of a friend.

Get your assistant to put the posts out twenty-five yards apart to form a square. Hold onto your dog whilst your helper walks across the centre of the square, upwind of the dog and throws several well-handled articles towards the far side of the square, several yards apart.

Wait until your assistant is out of the way and positioned behind and downwind of your position before sending the dog in to find and retrieve some of the articles. Always finish the exercise before the dog has recovered all of the articles during early training sessions. As his concentration improves with each session, you can start to reduce the size of some of the articles until the dog is happily working for up to six minutes and being successful.

It is important that all of the articles are positioned in the top half of the square to teach the dog to move away and cover the whole square. It is a disadvantage to train the dog to find articles which are only a yard or two away from you.

The next stage is to get your friend to put out a search square in view of the dog, then take the dog away and do some other training such as heel work, recall, etc. Then return to the square and put the dog in to find and retrieve the articles. You can continue to remove the visual association of seeing the articles thrown into the square and increase the association with the four poles and your command.

Now a few hints and tips on search square training. It is helpful with some dogs if you have someone standing by the side of the square with a ball in his pocket in case the dog struggles to find articles or starts to lose motivation. All that this person needs to do is to throw the ball quickly into the square without the dog seeing it. Just as the dog is about to give up he suddenly comes across his reward and the subsequent game with his ball. Confidence and enthusiasm should then develop with each subsequent session. Use a few commands and encouragement as necessary. The more noise you make, the harder the dog will find it to concentrate on his task.

If the dog gets into the habit of dropping or mouthing articles as he retrieves then go back to the retrieve exercise to correct this. It is bad practice to attempt to apply the correction within the search square. Use your own articles as little as possible. The dog will never have to find articles bearing your own scent so don't train him to, otherwise he may be encouraged to start discriminating.

After the initial training process, try to hide the articles or use articles that blend into the ground so that the dog is in no way encouraged to use his eyes at all. Move around as little as possible whilst the dog is working, otherwise his attention to searching will be distracted. Try to restrict your movements to the downwind side(s) of the square to avoid your own body scent blowing into the area. Train on as many different types of terrain as possible so that the dog gains the necessary experience.

Tracking

Tracking is such a complex subject that to cover it adequately would require an entire book. A dog of any age can be trained to track but the best time to start is when the dog is quite young and before too much formal control training has started, particularly before any compulsion methods have been employed. I personally prefer to start all of my dogs on tracking between six and sixteen weeks of age when they are most willing to learn how to employ their natural instincts to my advantage.

Let us look at the requirements of a tracking dog. We want the dog to follow the path the tracklayer has taken over various types of terrain in all sorts of weather conditions, concentrating, exclusively on that task for up to about half an hour and recovering any articles that may have been dropped. Because it is necessary for the dog to want to get round the track and want to recover articles we can only successfully train the dog using a system of reward.

Sadly many people fail to train their dogs to track successfully because they fail to teach the dog the correct association between using its nose to follow the track and subsequently finding articles. First consider the reward that you are going to use to teach your dog to track. How badly does he need the reward? Enough to exert himself both physically and mentally for up to half an hour?

Next consider where you are going to train him to track. Ideally you should start on a grass field with two to three inches of growth unfouled by people or animals walking over it for a couple of days prior to each training session. It would also be an advantage to have a friend who is also interested in track training to mutually assist you.

You will need a white post, pointed at one end, to indicate the commencement of the track, a well-fitting tracking harness, preferably leather, and a length of tracking line about twelve yards long with a good clip spliced onto one end for attaching to the harness.

I shall first describe the "classic" method of track training and then point out possible pitfalls that the novice handler can easily fall into.

Put the harness on the dog, attach the line, but fasten the other end to a fence post, etc. Push the tracking post into the ground at the extremity of the dog's movement the line allows him. Tease him with a toy then walk backwards directly into the wind, dragging your feet as you go, to put a continuous line of scent on the ground. After about twenty yards tease him with the toy and then place it on the ground. Return to the dog down the same line of track, unfasten the line and allow the dog to move forward and "track" to recover the toy. After several such sessions, a few dogs will learn that by following the scent on the ground they will find the toy; most will not have learnt to track at all! Of course they must have learned something during the training sessions because they find the toy every time.

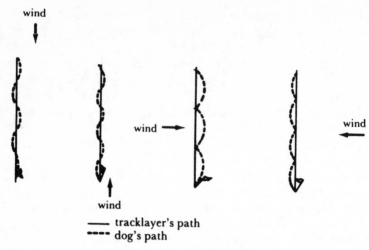

—— tracklayer's path
▪▪▪▪ dog's path

Figure 10   *Straight-line tracking*

A few dogs (mainly Dobermanns, Weimeraners and various gundogs) will have learnt to rush forward with their
noses in the air and pick up the scent of the ball on the
wind not even noticing that there is any significant smell on
the ground. A few dogs (Border Collies and Retrievers) will
have simply watched you walk away and "marked" the position of the toy visually and will run out using their visual
memory to get close to the toy then possibly search to locate
it.

Quite a number of dogs will have learnt to take instructions
from the handler as to the location of the toy and will therefore learn to rely on the handler taking them round the
track to find the reward.

A few dogs (German Shepherd Dogs, for instance) will be
so pleased that the owner has returned after walking a short
distance away and teasing, that they are not interested in
finding the toy at all but merely jump and fuss around the
handler not wanting to leave him.

So how can we eliminate all of the possible ways that the
dog can find the toy except by using his nose to follow the
track on the ground.

If, after the initial training session, you feel that the dog
is wind scenting, then lay all early straight-line tracks immedi-

ately downwind. Now the dog will find it impossible to wind scent the toy and is more likely to track. To prevent the dog marking the position of the toy visually, it can be dragged along the ground so that it disappears from the dog's sight within a few yards. Continue walking several yards beyond it before returning, so the dog has no chance of knowing where the toy is visually and will be more likely to concentrate on sniffing the ground to find it.

How about the handler that inadvertently leads his dog to the toy by walking down the line of track himself, preventing the dog from deviating. The best way here is to get a second person to lay the track, allowing the dog to watch but not the handler, who stands with his back to the post. Now the dog can only find the toy using his own ability to track and learns to become completely independent of his handler. This also prevents the dog being so pleased to see his handler return after laying the track that he becomes disinterested in tracking for the toy.

For the first few tracking sessions it is best to stick to straight-line tracks, extending the distance in stages up to about two hundred yards, satisfying yourself that the dog is in fact tracking all the way to the toy. At the completion of each track, remove harness and line and play with the toy. If the dog is not keen enough to want to find the toy, increase the dog's desire to play with the toy (see Chapter 3, "Training and Learning, page 86) before continuing tracking training. As an alternative to a toy you could use food instead – see free tracking.

Teach the dog to follow the track both into wind (not if the dog tends to wind scent) and downwind. At the next few sessions try working tracks laid crosswind and watch the path that the dog takes in trying to follow the scent. He will probably work these tracks in a series of steps until he gains experience. You will now need to start altering your training at each session to build up the associations in the dog's mind in order to prepare him for the conditions he is likely to meet in competition. The following list of training progression can be worked through in virtually any order once the dog has mastered straight-line tracks as above.

1. Tracking harness and tracking post have to be the primary associations.
2. We must progress from double-layed tracks, i.e., track-layer walks out and returns along the same line, to single-line track where the tracklayer does not return along the original line of track.
3. We must remove all visual stimuli at the start of the tracking session, i.e. tracklayer teasing the dog with the toy/food and walking away.
4. We have to "age" tracks, that is progressively teach the dog to follow a smaller amount of available scent on the ground.
5. We must teach the dog to indicate to the handler that he has found an article.
6. The handler must learn to use the line to the dog's advantage.
7. We must give the dog enough experience on various terrains and in variable weather conditions.
8. We must teach the dog to change direction on corners.
9. We need to increase the track length, in stages.
10. We need to teach the dog to follow the track even if crossed by livestock and game.

How can we achieve all of this? Well, taking the list in the order it is written you will hopefully have a much clearer picture in your mind before you start training seriously.

1. By placing the harness on only at the start of the track, a few yards from the pole, and removing it as soon as the dog has completed the track and before playing retrieve or tug-of-war on the toy, the dog should have a happy association with the harness and line. Commands to track are totally unnecessary and distracting for the dog.

2. Part of the dog's association with the commencement of the track is to watch the tracklayer return and pass him. As his experience starts to grow he will start moving forward past the tracklayer, almost disregarding him.

The first time a single-line track is laid the tracklayer should continue walking for ten paces or so, turn at 90 degrees to the left or right and walk in a large semi-circle to end up behind dog and handler. When this happens quite a few dogs want to head off in the direction he has returned from (back tracking) because of this prior association. To eliminate this happening simply get the tracklayer to walk ten paces or so past the tracking post, down the line of track, about-turn and walk back past the dog to maintain the previous associations. The dog will now definitely start in the correct direction. Over the next few sessions you can reduce the number of yards that the tracklayer relays at the start until the dog gets the idea that the post indicates the commencement of the track and thus disregards the direction from which the tracklayer has returned.

3. We must also progressively train the dog to follow a blind track, that is, a track that has been laid out of sight of the dog. Start by letting the dog watch the tracklayer push the tracking post into the ground, then tease the dog with the reward and walk away to lay the track. After the tracklayer has walked about twenty-five yards take the dog out of the field, behind a hedge, fence, etc., out of sight of the tracklayer. When the tracklayer has finished laying the track tell him to return to the post and stand next to it. Bring the dog into the field, put on his harness and line, have the tracklayer walk back from the post past you. The dog should immediately put his nose down and track. You can then progress to holding the dog at the entrance to the field, let him watch the tracklayer walk into the field with a post and the dog's reward. Keep the dog out of sight of the track being laid. As soon as the tracklayer comes back out of the field, take the dog up, close to the pole, put on the harness and line and let him start the track. The last stage is to have a track laid whilst the dog is completely out of sight and has no idea that it is being laid. Just before you run the track let the dog watch your tracklayer walk towards the field, disappearing out of sight, with a white post and a reward similar to the one he has put at the end of the track. The tracklayer should then put the reward, out of of sight, into his pocket and hide the post against the fence. Take the dog into the field to within a few yards of the post at the start of the track, put on his harness and line, and you will have

no problems with him starting the track. You can continue this association right up to and including your first few trials. The dog's mind is firmly fixed on tracking before he even gets into the field!

4. Once the dog has mastered the initial tracking process you can start to reduce the amount of available scent on the ground by walking instead of dragging your feet. The problem with trying to teach the dog progressively to follow smaller amounts of scent is that you can only use elapsed time as a basis if terrain and weather conditions remain unchanged at each and every training session. Because of the variables over which you have no control it becomes almost impossible to train progressively. You may well run a track two hours old this week under good tracking condition and without problems, but may struggle to get round a half-hour track under poor conditions next week. For novices the problems are greater; what are good and bad conditions? Only experience can give you that information and even then the "experts" often get it wrong.

There is a way, however, that you can get a good indication of the amount of scent in order to assist in training the dog. Just follow these instructions:

a) Lay a track for the dog.
b) Lay a straight line from a post approximately fifty yards in length with an article at the end. This must be laid in the same field as the main track but not interfering with it, and laid straight after.
c) Lay a second and third straight line as above.
d) Make an assessment of prevailing weather conditions.
e) Run the first fifty-yard track any "age" you desire and note how the dog works it. If the dog charges along without really having to concentrate, wait a further length of time. Run the second fifty-yard track and again assess the dog's performance. If he has to concentrate quite hard to stay on line of track and is unable to deviate far from the actual line, wait a few minutes and then run the main track. If he charges along without concentrating and is able to detect the track at a distance from the

actual line wait a while and run the third fifty-yard leg, repeating as above.

Let us imagine that you have made an error of judgement, and when you put the dog on the fifty-yard leg he has extreme difficulty in finding and following the track. He only has fifty yards to go before finding the article and finishing successfully. Do not run the main track at all, it will only defeat the dog and damage his (and your) confidence. You can see that it is possible to give the dog experience on progressively harder tracks if you wish without making anything either too difficult or too easy all of the time.

5. Articles. The indication a dog gives that it has found an article must be clear to both judge and handler. A few handlers get the dog to retrieve the article, but this sometimes presents a problem where small articles are located in long grass for if the dog drops the article on its way back to the handler the chances are the article will be lost.

The two most favoured methods are teaching the dog to stand over the article or to lie down. A point that I should make here is that you must not use any compulsion to teach article indication otherwise the dog may well try to avoid articles and the subsequent compulsion. You will have started the dog tracking using some form of reward such as a toy or food. The next stage is to lay a track with four or five largish articles about the size of a cartridge case or matchbox evenly spaced along the last part of the track at twenty-yard intervals, the reward being twenty yards beyond the last article. If you get any indication at all stop the dog, go up and investigate. Make a big fuss of him, remove the harness and either play with the article or pretend to find food inside it for him depending on how you carried out the initial training. Don't worry if the dog completely misses the articles. After a few sessions the dog should associate the same enjoyable experience of finding his reward with finding articles. When you are happy that the dog is locating articles you can either use the line to teach the dog to stand until you get up to recover the article or teach the dog to lie down. Go up and gently push the dog into the down position before picking the article up for a game or feeding him from it. You can then space the articles out more evenly along the length of the track, but always place the rewards twenty yards after the last article just in case the dog misses them. Progress to smaller articles and varying materials in order to give the dog valuable experience.

6. Line handling. This can be one of the most difficult areas for a beginner to understand, and the best way of learning is to go and watch the way experienced handlers use the tracking line to the dog's advantage. The old days of the handler maintaining his position at the extremity of the line throughout the duration of the track are a thing of the past. Most of the top handlers maintain a position within a few yards of the dog, letting the excess line trail behind them. That extra line is used on corners to allow the dog to change direction without the handler having to move until he is certain that the dog is tracking correctly. The handler then moves back up the line until he regains his position behind the dog. Indications of articles and corners are to see if you are close to the dog. The problem is that no two dogs are the same, and so only experience in handling your individual dog will tell you how far behind him you should walk.

7. Terrain and Weather. It is important that the dog is given the experience to cope with various types of terrain such as grassland, ploughed fields, growing corn, heather, moorland scrub, stubble fields and pasture. Each time you introduce your dog to a new tracking surface, go back to basic straight-line tracks until the dog builds up confidence. Each surface has its own peculiarities, and one of the difficulties every handler is faced with is gaining access to various types of tracking ground.

One thing that you will quite definitely need if you intend to take tracking seriously is a good set of waterproof clothing, because it is important to train the dog to cope with weather conditions that he may expect in competition. Once again the rule is to train progressively. The first track you attempt in pouring rain should be run quite fresh, as should first tracks on snow, in high winds, blazing sunshine, etc. Don't cancel training if the weather is bad, use it to your advantage.

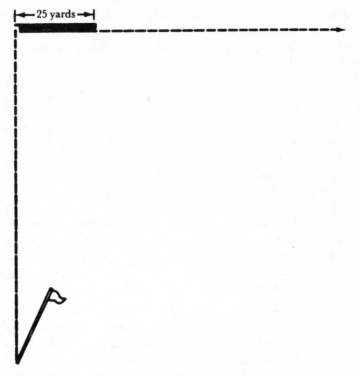

Figure 11 *Triple laying*

8. Corners. Once the dog has mastered straight-line tracks to your satisfaction you are ready to start training corners. The best way of doing this is to have your tracklayer start to lay the first leg of the track in sight of the dog for about twenty-five yards, then turn the dog around so that he cannot see. The tracklayer then continues for a further twenty-five yards in a straight line before turning through 90 degrees to left or right, either directly into the wind or downwind depending on whether the dog has a tendency to wind scent or not. After another twenty-five yards in the new direction the tracklayer should about-turn and walk back along the second leg of the track for a distance of about forty yards before putting the reward down. This is known as triple laying.

The tracklayer then curves back towards the handler and

dog, keeping well clear of the track. As soon as the tracklayer is positioned behind the handler, the dog is turned around and allowed to start the track. When he reaches the corner he will lose the track, possibly overshooting by several yards. When he indicates to you that he has lost the track (and not before), stand still and let him cast around. As soon as he is anywhere near the next leg he should take a new direction quite confidently as there is plenty of scent on the triple-laid portion. After moving twenty-five yards the scent thins out, but by this time the dog should be moving quite confidently. He now only has to travel a further fifteen yards on the single-line track before finishing by finding the reward.

Continue by giving the dog experience on corners into the wind, downwind. crosswind, etc., and then reduce the number of yards of triple laying in stages until the dog confidently changes direction on a single-line track. You can then introduce acute angles, increase the number of legs, etc., to give the dog more experience.

9. Increasing length of track. The general rule is to increase the track length on fresh simple tracks of no more than three legs in order to build up concentration. You can increase track length from 200 yards up to 1000 yards over several sessions provided the dog is highly motivated. It is a good plan to place several articles on the track evenly spaced when you start increasing length, just in case the dog starts to tire and lose concentration whereupon you can finish on the next article without pushing the dog beyond its limits. Never increase both the track length, age and number of legs at the same sessions. Build up each aspect of tracking individually.

10. If the dog has been brought up with livestock, few problems should be encountered with game or livestock crosstracks. If, however, the dog is distracted, the best plan is to run tracks in fields alongside those which contain sheep, horses, cattle, etc., so that the dog gets used to the background smell and will be less likely to take too much interest when the novelty value wears off.

If, however, the dog becomes over excited, preferring to follow the scent of game or livestock rather than the tracklayer's path you will need to apply some correction.

You should take the dog out, quite separately from tracking training and walk him in fields where livestock and/ or game have been. Each time he starts to put his nose down to smell or even eat any animal droppings, apply some compulsion such as throwing a plastic lemonade bottle at him or growling at him depending on how sensitive he is. If he finds the experience of sniffing where any animals have been a completely unrewarding experience he will quickly become disinterested. Now you can go back to track training.

Free tracking

I personally favour a system of training young dogs (six to sixteen weeks) to track independently of their handlers. At this tender age it is possible to get the dog to concentrate for long on a toy and so food is the best way of motivating the dog.

The initial training spans about ten consecutive days where the puppy learns to track for its dinner each day as follows. Mix the pup's food up at it's mealtime and tease him with it, but don't let him touch it. Wait for half an hour or so and then take him out to the tracking area with his bowl of food. Hold on to the pup and get an assistant to walk backwards away from the pup dragging the bowl along the ground. The assistant should leave the bowl about fifteen yards away, out of sight of the dog and walk back along the same line of track. As soon as the tracklayer is behind you, release the pup.

He may not move towards the food at all initially but will go through a sequence of behaviours to try and find the food. He may well jump up at the tracklayer – ignore him. He may jump up at the handler and cry – ignore him. Give him a minute or so, and if he makes no effort to track repeat the procedure letting your assistant re-motivate the dog by teasing him with the food as many times as necessary until the dog finds and eats its. A word of caution here; if you are not blessed with a great deal of patience then wait until the pup is older and teach it on a harness and line.

If you persist you will end up with a dog that after a few

sessions is enjoying the opportunity of tracking for his dinner. You can extend the track length up to about fifty yards in a straight line, satisfying yourself that the dog is tracking to get to his food. Then lay a corner as described earlier, but only have the tracklayer return down the same line of track. Release the dog and watch him. When he loses the track he will start to gallop around in a big wide arc. If he happens to hit the new direction he will continue along the track and recover the food. If he dashes around and does not hit the new line of track he may well come back to you. Ignore him for a few minutes. If he comes to a complete standstill repeat the process until he is successful. As soon as he is cornering confidently, add a second corner. Once the dog has mastered this you can now reduce his movement on corners by using a harness and line.

Over a period of ten to twenty days most dogs will have learnt to track quite independently of their owners and to change direction to obtain the reward. This is an advantage in later life as the dog will never rely on its handler for assistance if it gets into difficulty but will rely on its own ability. My own dog Xandoa's Quaver, C.D.ex, U.D.ex, W.D.ex, T.D.ex, P.D.ex, got his Open Tracking Dog Certificate (three-hour-old track, half a mile long recovering three articles) at eleven months of age using just this system of training.

The preceding pages should at least give an insight into the fascinating subject of tracking but are for guidance only. Even the most comprehensive book yet written on the subject is no substitute for practical sessions under the instruction of the many professional and semi-professional trainers who specialize in this type of training.

Agility

Training a dog to jump can be an enjoyable experience for both dog and handler if it is carried out correctly. Unfortunately some dogs hate the jumps if they have a disagreeable experience with them in early training. It is important that you have an experienced trainer in attendance at all early agility training sessions to minimize mistakes and possible injury.

The dog must be in good athletic condition, well-muscled and not overweight. He must also be old enough for his limbs to take the stresses involved in jumping. This varies from breed to breed and dog to dog. The best bet is to get your vet to check the dog prior to commencement of training. If you own a breed that is prone to hip displasia, get it X-rayed before starting agility training.

The agility equipment should be painted to be clearly visible, with the exception of scale jumps and A-frames which should have the contact surfaces left natural to allow the dog traction. Clear jumps for training purposes should have a top bar which knocks off to prevent the dog hurting himself and to prevent him getting into the habit of exerting pressure on the top bar. This can easily happen if solid training jumps are used. All training equipment must be capable of being lowered to give the dog confidence and build up the association with commands.

Once again there are two methods of training. The dog can be made to jump or encouraged to want to jump. Only ever concern yourself with making the dog want to jump. There are three different techniques required for agility training: 1) the dog making physical contact with the jump to pull himself over 2) the dog jumping with a low trajectory to maintain maximum speed (agility competitions) and 3) jumping to gain maximum height and distance over the obstacle (working trials)

These brief notes may assist you to teach your dog each of the techniques.

Scale jump/A-frame

It is always easier to start by teaching the dog to jump towards you for a reward rather than jumping away from you, particularly if the jump is going to obscure his vision (recall is always easier that sendaway). Get your experienced assistant to hold the dog on a lead, go to the other side of the jump, tease him with a toy or food and call and encourage the dog to come towards you. Your assistant merely prevents the dog coming round the jump. The only way to reach you is by jumping. As soon as the dog makes the correct decision the assistant simply lets go of the lead.

The jump is increased in height very quickly to a height where the dog does not even think of jumping to clear it but runs or scrambles up it. If the dog has difficulty when the jump nears it maximum height your assistant is there to prevent the dog falling back risking injury.

As the dog's confidence grows and his technique improves you can place a reward on the far side of the obstacle and teach him to jump away from you. With the scale jump, the control position, sit, stand or down, is trained separately and independently of the jump.

With the agility A-frame, placing food or a toy at the foot of the jump on the far side will maintain the contact points.

Low trajectory jumping (agility)

In order to teach the dog to maintain a low trajectory over the jumps, start off with several jumps set at a very low level in a straight line at random and uneven distances apart. Teach the dog to judge distance and height and to alter his stride pattern before increasing the height of any jump. Then increase the height slowly on all of the jumps until he can successfully judge take-off distance and height from several yards away from each jump in the line.

Clear jump and long jump (trials)

These jumps are carried out to achieve maximum height and distance without any contact with the jump.

To achieve this it is important that the dog is positioned accurately in front of the jump. He must also be at the correct distance away to allow him to accelerate and reach the jump on the correct leg for take off, and so that his take off landing positions are equi-distant from the centre of the jump so that he attains maximum height at the centre of the jump. Watch an athlete doing a high jump or long jump and you will see what I mean. Take off too far back from the jump and you will hit it going down; too close and you will hit it going up. The distance the dog is sent from is individual to each dog, and to find the correct distance get a helper to stand by the side of the jump and mark the dog's take off and landing positions. Keep adjusting the dog's run up until the dog's take off and landing positions are correct. Measure this distance and always use it to position the dog when jumping him.

Happy training!

Appendix A

If you are having problems with your dog either related to training or behaviour then my recommendation is that you make an appointment with one of my associates listed below. All are experienced in training and applied dog behaviour, charge a fixed fee and are committed to help and improve the relationships that people have with their pets.

John Rogerson and Associates

Alasdair Bunyan
2 Dampark,
Dunlop,
Ayreshire,
Scotland KA3 4BZ
Tel: 01560 483669

Elaine Hemingway
87 Bradford Road,
Brighouse,
West Yorkshire HD6 4AD
Tel: 01474 384852

Mary Owens
Fircroft Kennels
Cappanargid,
Rathangan,
Co. Kildare
Tel: 045 524250

Steve Collis
Flat Two,
19 Hugh Mews,
London SW1V 1QH
Tel/Fax: 0171 828 9438

David Bates
4 Gravelhill Road,
Maze,
Lisburn,
Co. Antrim
N. Ireland
Tel: 0846 622038

Dolores Palmer
25 Speechley Drive,
Rugeley,
Staffs.
Tel: 01889 579103

Carla Nieuwenhuizen
Ryelands House,
Aynho,
Banbury,
Oxon OX17 3AT
Tel: 01869 810646

Jane Sharp
3 Azalea Way,
George Green,
Nr. Slough,
Bucks. SL3 6RL
Tel: 01753 536861
E.Mail: jane.sharp@virgin.net

Lorraine Margiotta
The Bungalow,
Beckingham Road,
Coddington,
Newark,

Notts. NG24 2QS
Tel: 01636 702012
E. Mail: lorraine.margiotta@virgin.net

Nicola James
The Dower House,
Bonsall,
Derbyshire DE4 2AR
Tel: 01629 822137

John Rogerson
The Northern Centre for Animal Behaviour
East Howle,
Ferryhill,
Durham DL17 8SA
Tel: 01740 653572
E.Mail: 101652,103@compuserve.comu